The Revolution of the Dialectic

THE REVOLUTION OF THE DIALECTIC

ESOTERIC PSYCHOLOGY AND MEDITATION: PRACTICAL METHODS FOR INTENSE SPIRITUAL TRANSFORMATION

Samael Aun Weor

GLORIAN
2010

The Revolution of the Dialectic
Christmas Message 1972-1973
A Glorian Book / 2010

Originally published in Spanish as "La Revolucion de la
Dialectica" (1983).

This Edition © 2010 Glorian Publishing

ISBN 978-1-934206-42-3

Library of Congress Control Number: 2006908906

Glorian Publishing (formerly Thelema Press) is a non-profit
organization delivering to humanity the teachings of Samael Aun
Weor. All proceeds go to further the distribution of these books.
For more information, visit our website.

glorian.info
gnosticbooks.org
gnosticteachings.org
gnosticradio.org
gnosticschool.org
gnosticstore.org
gnosticvideos.org

Contents

Prologue

The mind-heart of the Intellectual Animal (called "human being" out of sympathy) is full of vain theories and mental suppositions, which cannot lead us to anything positive.

Modern intellectuals want to make a new world in accord with the fantastic model that they have built within their minds.

Leader politicians with the purpose of gaining power make astonishing promises to the suffering and starving multitudes; however, once their ambition is satisfied, they broadly laugh at the expense of the wretched, imbecilic populace.

The world is in crisis and everywhere there are wars and rumors of wars, promises and mockeries, bombardments and political parties that mutually combat each other.

It is absurd to suppose that we can depart from this social chaos with all of its fights and miseries, if indeed, individually, we do not resolve ourselves to perform a radical and definitive change.

Useless are the legal or illegal changes of governments, the bloody dictatorships, the revolutions of blood and alcohol. If we truly want an absolutely radical change, then first of all, we need to change ourselves individually.

What we are as individuals is what the world is. Indeed, the world is the individual, because the world is nothing more than the sum of all individuals. The problem of the world is the problem of the individual. Thus, if the individual does not internally change, then the world will never change either, even when many want to change it based on extremist doctrines, bloody revolutions, abominable dictatorships, etc.

If we study our intimate problems in detail, then we have to arrive at the logical conclusion that no leader can resolve these problems for us. What I am, is in fact, the party, the group, the family, the society, the nation.

The individual is the beginning and the ending of every order of things. Thus, if we want a radical transformation of this bitter and suffering world, then we need each of us to individually transform ourselves in a true and very intimate way.

We need with an expedited urgency to firmly establish within our mind the positive values of the spirit.

When the coarse values of the world inhabit our minds, then the outcome is starvation, misery, war, ignorance, sicknesses, etc.

Only based on profound comprehension can we resolve in a positive and true way all the economical and social problems of the world that afflict and torture us.

Oppression and exploitation, the aggressiveness and economical cruelty of these times, are due to the absence of the eternal values of the spirit.

Darkness is never dissolved with hand's blows, but with the light. An error cannot be dissolved by combating it with violence, but by teaching the truth.

Therefore, political doctrines that are established by means of violence will never achieve the end of dictatorships, greed, ambition, egotism, and incompetence.

When the law restricts the human being, then he looks for substitutes, for his own personal satisfaction. Those substitutes become vehicles of our own mistakes, hatred, egotism, jealousy, ambitions, etc.. This is how new dictatorships are mocked.

In the end, the Czar and his royal family in Russia were substituted by Lenin, Stalin, Khrushchev, and the entire Kremlin company. Individual capitalism was substituted by the capitalism of the state and the old bourgeoisie was replaced by the new bourgeoisie, disguised as Proletarian. Thus, in Russia, all the old ambitions were disguised with the doctrine of Marx and Lenin. All the vices and evilness were multiplied in secrecy, and cruelty became gruesome because of the lack of the eternal values.

If indeed we love humanity, if we want to cooperate in the initiation of the new era that is beginning, then it is necessary for an intimate and intelligent transformation to happen voluntarily within each individual.

Surely, this intimate change cannot be produced by means of any type of exterior violence or coactions, because if that would happen, then new social and bitter disasters would be the outcome of it. Intimate regeneration must be voluntary, intelligent, and never obligatory.

We must be sincere with ourselves and make a dissection of the "I" with the tremendous scalpel of self-criticism.

It is absurd to criticize the errors of a neighbor. What is fundamental is to discover our own errors and to disintegrate them based on analysis and very profound comprehension.

When an error has been totally comprehended in an integral way and in all of the deepest levels of the mind, it is inevitably disintegrated.

This is how we can dissolve the "I." Only with the death of the "I" can we make a better world.

We need to liberate the mind and heart from any type of evilness if we truly want to transform ourselves intimately for the good of the world.

dialectic: discussion and reasoning by dialogue as a method to resolve disagreement and reveal the truth

Reflection

Our position is absolutely independent. The revolution of the dialectic does not have any weapons other than intelligence, neither systems other than wisdom.

The new culture will be synthetic, and its base will be the revolution of the dialectic.

This book is eminently practical, essentially ethical and profoundly dialectical, philosophical, and scientific.

It does not matter to science or to us whether there are some who laugh at this book, criticize us or if they insult us; for "the one who laughs at what he does not know is an ignoramus that walks on the path of idiocy."

Now, here comes this treatise upon the battlefield, like a terrible lion that unmasks the traitors and disconcerts the tyrants before the solemn verdict of public consciousness.

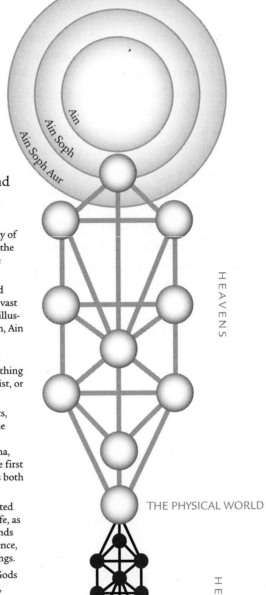

Our Inner Being and the Kabbalah - The Tree of Life

Monotheism (the Theology of the One) and Polytheism (the Theology of the Many) are synthesized in Kabbalah.

God as One, the Uncreated Light or Emptiness, is the vast potentiality for existence, illustrated here [top] as the Ain, Ain Soph, Ain Soph Aur.

When creation occurs, the No-thing emerges as One-thing (the Light, also called Christ, or the Ray of Creation).

This light has three aspects, known as the Tri-unity; the Trinity (Father, Son, Holy Spirit) or Trimurti (Brahma, Vishnu, Shiva). This is the first or Supernal Triangle. It is both One and Three.

The Law of Three is reflected throughout the Tree of Life, as the Ray of Creation descends into denser levels of existence, ultimately creating all things.

Every great Pantheon of Gods and Goddesses (or Angels, Devas, etc.) can be "mapped" onto the Tree of Life, thereby revealing the intelligent principles that manifest and organize creation on every level.

HEAVENS

THE PHYSICAL WORLD

HELLS

Ain

Ain Soph

Ain Soph Aur

The Revolution of the Dialectic

Monotheism always leads to anthropomorphism (idolatry), which by reaction originates materialistic atheism. This is why we prefer polytheism.

We are not afraid to talk about the intelligent principles of the mechanical phenomena of nature, even if people classify us as pagans.

We are partisans of a modern polytheism founded on Psychotronics.

In final synthesis, monotheistic doctrines lead to idolatry. It is preferable to talk about intelligent principles, which never leads to materialism.

In turn, the abuse of polytheism, by reaction, leads to monotheism.

Modern monotheism emerged from the abuse of polytheism.

In this era of Aquarius, in this new phase of the revolution of the dialectic, polytheism must be psychologically and transcendentally sketched out. Besides, it must be put forward intelligently; we must set forth wisely with a vital and integral monistic polytheism.

Monistic polytheism is the synthesis of polytheism and monotheism. Diversity is unity.

In the revolution of the dialectic, the terms good and evil, evolution and devolution, God or religion are not used.

In these decrepit and degenerate times, a revolution of the dialectic, a self-dialectic, and a new education are necessary.

In the age of the revolution of the dialectic, the art of reasoning must be handled directly by our Inner Being in order for it to be methodical and just. An art of Objective Reasoning will provide a pedagogical and integral change.

All the actions of our life must be the outcome of an equation and an exact formula in order for the possibilities of the mind and the functionalism of understanding to surge forth.

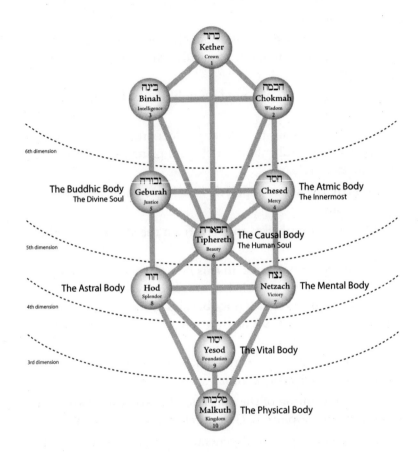

THE SEVEN BODIES ON THE TREE OF LIFE

The revolution of the dialectic has the precise clue in order to create an emancipated and unitotal mind; this is the clue to form minds free of conditioning, free of conceptual options.

The revolution of the dialectic does not have dictatorial norms for the mind.

The revolution of the dialectic does not seek to abuse intellectual liberty.

The revolution of the dialectic wants to teach *how* one should think.

The revolution of the dialectic does not want to cage or imprison thought.

The revolution of the dialectic wants the integration of all the values of the human being.

The Teachings

Only life intensely lived provides lasting wisdom. However, the mind, which is the one that causes us to commit errors, impedes us from arriving at the amphitheatre of cosmic science. The errors of the mind are those "'I's" or psychological defects that the intellectual animal, falsely called a human being, carries within his interior.

The psychological defects are within the 49 levels of our consciousness.

We cannot recognize or find the "'I's" or egos of the 49 subconscious levels, because each one of them has parts of themselves within our different bodies. To know them, we must appeal to a force that is superior to the mind, so that this force may disintegrate them. This force is our Divine Mother Kundalini; she will disintegrate them with her serpentine fire.

Only the Mother Kundalini of Hindu mysteries knows the 49 levels of our subconsciousness.

The studied psychological defects do not form part of our Being. This is why after having studied the psychologi-

LEFT: (HINDUISM) THE DIVINE MOTHER IN THE FORM OF DURGA SLAYS THE DEMON OF DESIRE AND IGNORANCE.
RIGHT: (GRECO-ROMAN) THE DIVINE MOTHER IN THE FORM OF ATHENA (MINERVA) WITH HER SERPENT.
ATHENA EMPOWERS THE HEROIC HUMAN SOUL TO DESTROY HER ANTITHESIS (MEDUSA, MINOTAUR, ETC)

cal defect through meditation one supplicates **Ram-Io** (the Mother Kundalini) to disintegrate it with the sexual energy during Sexual Super-dynamics.

We cannot get to see a defect in the mind by means of the intellect and reflection. Everyone remains stagnant there because we do not know the other seven bodies of the mind. It is there that the ego has its den.

The mind, the intellect, the reasoning (and all the more subjective methods with which the human being works) can never reach the profound levels of subconsciousness, which is where the ego continuously develops its film and makes the consciousness slumber. Only the Kundalini, with its sexual fire, can reach the 49 levels in order to definitely disintegrate that which causes us pain; that which holds us in misery; that which people painfully love; that which present materialistic psychology has wanted to deify; that which is called ego, which the revolution of the dialectic wants to destroy in order to achieve an integral revolution.

Chapter I

The Didactic for the
Dissolution of the "I"

The best didactic for the dissolution of the "I" is found in an intensely lived practical life.

Interrelationships are a marvelous full length mirror in which the "I" can be thoroughly contemplated.

In relationships with our fellowmen, the defects that are hidden flourish spontaneously from within the depths of our subconsciousness. The defects leap out because our subconsciousness betrays us. Only if we are in a state of alert perception can we see them as they really are.

For the Gnostic, the greatest joy and celebration comes from the discovery of one of his defects, because that discovered defect will become a dead defect. When we discover a defect, we must view it much like someone who is watching a scene from a movie, but we must not condemn or justify it.

It is not enough to intellectually comprehend the psychological defect. It is necessary to submerge ourselves into profound inner meditation in order to catch the defect in all the levels of the mind.

The mind has many levels and profundities. If we have not comprehended a defect in all the levels of the mind then we have done nothing. Therefore, that defect will continue to exist like a tempting demon in the depths of our own subconsciousness.

When a defect is integrally comprehended in all the levels of the mind, then that defect disintegrates and the "I" which characterizes it is reduced to cosmic dust.

This is how we keep on dying from moment to moment. This is how we keep establishing within ourselves a Permanent Center of Consciousness, a center of permanent gravity.

The Buddhadatu, the Buddhist principle, exists within the interior of every human being who is not yet in the final state of degeneration. This Buddhadatu is the psychic material or raw material that can be fabricated into what is called a Soul.

The pluralized "I" foolishly spends such psychic material in absurd atomic explosions of envy, covetousness, hatred, jealousy, fornication, attachments, vanity, etc.

As the pluralized "I" dies from moment to moment, the psychic material accumulates within us, thus becoming a Permanent Center of Consciousness.

This is how we individualize ourselves little by little. By de-egotizing ourselves, we individualize ourselves. However, we must clarify that individuality is not everything; with the event of Bethlehem we must move onto super-individuality.

The work of the dissolution of the "I" is something very serious. We need to study ourselves profoundly in all the levels of the mind. The "I" is a book of many chapters.

We need to study our dialectic, our thoughts, our emotions, our actions from moment to moment, without justifying or condemning them. We need to integrally comprehend each and every one of our defects in all the profundities of our mind.

The pluralized "I" is the subconsciousness. When we dissolve the "I," the subconsciousness becomes consciousness.

We need to convert the subconsciousness into consciousness. This is only possible by achieving the annihilation of the "I."

When the consciousness moves on to occupy the place of the subconsciousness, we then acquire that which is called continuous consciousness.

The one who enjoys continuous consciousness lives consciously in every moment, not only in the physical world but also in the superior worlds.

This present humanity is ninety-seven percent subconscious. This is why humanity sleeps profoundly in both the physical world and the supra-sensible worlds, not only during the sleep of the physical body, but also after death.

We need the death of the "I." We need to die from moment to moment, here and now, not only in the physical world, but in all the planes of the Cosmic Mind as well.

We must be merciless towards ourselves and carry out the dissection of the "I" with the great scalpel of self-criticism.

The Struggle of the Opposites

A great master once said, "Seek enlightenment, for all else will be added onto you."

Enlightenment's worst enemy is the "I." It is necessary to know that the "I" is a knot in the flow of existence, a fatal obstruction in the flow of life free in its movement.

A master was asked, "What is the way?"

"What a magnificent mountain!" he said, referring to the mountain where he had his haven.

"I am not asking you about the mountain; instead, I am asking you about the path."

"As long as you cannot go beyond the mountain, you will not be able to find the path," answered the master.

Another monk asked the same question to that same master.

"There it is, right before your eyes," the master answered him.

"Why can I not see it?"

"Because you have egotistical ideas."

"Will I be able to see it, sir?"

"As long as you have dualistic vision and you say, 'I cannot' and so on, your eyes will be blinded by that relative vision."

"When there is no I or you, can it be seen?"

"When there is no I or you, who wants to see it?"

The foundation of the "I" is the dualism of the mind. The "I" is sustained by the battle of the opposites.

All thinking is based upon the battle of the opposites. If we say such person is tall, we want to say that she is not short. If we say that we are entering, we want to say that we are not exiting. If we say that we are happy, with that we affirm that we are not sad, etc.

The problems of life are nothing more than mental forms with two poles: one positive and the other negative. Problems are sustained by the mind and are created by the mind. When we stop thinking about a problem, inevitably the latter ends.

Happiness and sadness; pleasure and pain; good and evil; victory and defeat; these constitute the battle of the opposites upon which the "I" is rooted.

We live our entire miserable life going from one extreme to another: victory, defeat; like, dislike; pleasure, pain; failure, success; this, that, etc.

We need to free ourselves from the tyranny of the opposites. This is only possible by learning how to live from moment to moment without any type of abstractions, without any dreams and without any fantasies.

Hast thou observed how the stones on the road are pale and pure after a torrential rain? One can only murmur an "Oh!" of admiration. We must comprehend that "Oh!" of things without deforming that divine exclamation with the battle of the opposites.

Joshu asked the master Nansen, "What is the TAO?"

"Ordinary life," replied Nansen.

"What does one do in order to live in accordance with it?"

"If you try to live in accordance with it, then it will flee away from you; do not try to sing that song; let it be sung by itself. Does not the humble hiccup come by itself?"

Remember this phrase: "Gnosis is lived upon facts, withers away in abstractions, and is difficult to find even in the noblest of thoughts."

They asked the master Bokujo, "Do we have to dress and eat daily? How can we escape from this?"

The master replied, "We eat, we get dressed."

"I do not comprehend," said the disciple.

"Then get dressed and eat," said the master.

This is precisely action free of the opposites: Do we eat, do we get dressed? Why make a problem of that? Why think about other things while we are eating and getting dressed?

If you are eating, eat; if you are getting dressed, get dressed, and if you are walking on the street, walk, walk, walk, but do not think about anything else. Do only what you are doing. Do not run away from the facts; do not fill them with so many meanings, symbols, sermons and warnings. Live them without allegories. Live them with a receptive mind from moment to moment.

Comprehend that I am talking to you about the path of action, free of the painful battle of the opposites.

I am talking to you about action without distractions, without evasions, without fantasies, without abstractions of any kind.

Change thy character, beloved, change it through intelligent action, free of the battle of the opposites.

When the doors of fantasy are closed, the organ of intuition awakens.

Action, free of the battle of the opposites, is intuitive action, full action; for where there is plenitude, the "I" is absent.

Intuitive action leads us by the hand towards the awakening of the consciousness.

Let us work and rest happily, abandoning ourselves to the course of life. Let us exhaust the turbid and rotten waters of habitual thinking. Thus, into the emptiness Gnosis will flow, and with it, the happiness of living.

This intelligent action, free of the battle of the opposites, elevates us to a breaking point.

When everything is proceeding well, the rigid roof of thinking is broken. Then the light and power of the Inner Self floods the mind that has stopped dreaming.

Then in the physical world and beyond, while the material body sleeps, we live totally conscious and enlightened, enjoying the joys of life within the Superior Worlds.

This continuous tension of the mind, this discipline, takes us towards the awakening of the consciousness.

If we are eating and thinking about business, it is clear that we are dreaming. If we are driving an automobile and we are thinking about our fiancée, it is logical that we are not awake, we are dreaming; if we are working and we are remembering our child's godfather or godmother, or our friend, or brother, etc., it is clear that we are dreaming.

People who live dreaming in the physical world also live dreaming within the internal worlds (during those hours in which the physical body is asleep).

One needs to cease dreaming within the internal worlds. When we stop dreaming in the physical world, we awaken here and now, and that awakening appears in the internal worlds.

First seek enlightenment and all else will be added onto you.

Whosoever is enlightened sees the way; whosoever is not enlightened cannot see the way and can easily be led astray from the path and fall into the abyss.

Tremendous is the effort and the vigilance that is needed from second to second, from moment to moment, in order to not fall into illusions. One minute of unawareness is enough for the mind to be already dreaming about something else, distracting it from the job or deed that we are living at the moment.

When we are in the physical world, we learn to be awake from moment to moment. We then live awakened and self-conscious from moment to moment in the internal worlds, both during the hours of sleep of the physical body and also after death.

It is painful to know that the consciousness of all human beings sleeps and dreams profoundly not only during the hours of rest of the physical body, but also during that state ironically called the vigil state.

Action free of mental dualism produces the awakening of the consciousness.

The K-H

I have to declare before the solemn verdict of public opinion that the fundamental aim of every Gnostic student is to become a K-H: a Kosmos Human.

All of us human beings live in a Kosmos. We must never forget that the word *kosmos* means "order."

The Kosmos Human is a being who has perfect order in his five centers, in his mind, and in his Essence.

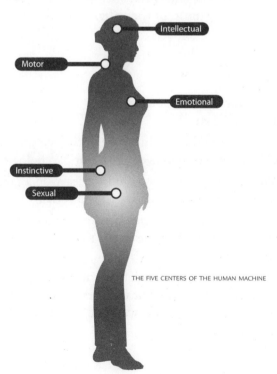

THE FIVE CENTERS OF THE HUMAN MACHINE

In order to become a Kosmos Human, it is necessary to learn how the Three Primary Forces of the universe—positive, negative and neutral—manifest themselves.

On the path that leads to the Kosmos Human (a path totally positive), we see that every positive force is always opposed by a negative force.

Through self-observation we must perceive the mechanism of the opposing force.

Whenever we propose to carry out a special action, whether it be annihilating an ego, controlling sexual energy, doing a special work, or executing a definite program, we must observe and calculate the force of resistance, because by nature the world and its mechanicity tends to provoke resistance and such resistance is doubled.

The more gigantic the enterprise, the greater the resistance will be. If we learn to calculate the resistance, we will also be able to develop the enterprise with success. This is where the capacity of the genius, of the enlightened one, is.

Resistance

Resistance is the opposing force. Resistance is the secret weapon of the ego.

Resistance is the psychic force of the ego that is opposed to us becoming conscious of all of our psychological defects.

With resistance, the ego tends to leave on a tangent and postulates excuses to silence or hide its error.

Due to resistance, dreams become difficult to interpret and the knowledge that one wants to have about oneself becomes clouded.

Resistance acts upon a defense mechanism that tries to omit unpleasant psychological errors, so as not to have consciousness of them. In this way, one continues in psychological slavery.

But, verily, I have to state that indeed there are mechanisms to overcome resistance. They are:

1. Recognize it
2. Define it
3. Comprehend it
4. Work on it
5. Overcome and disintegrate it by means of Sexual Super-dynamics

The ego will battle during the analysis of the resistance so that his fallacies are not discovered, because this analysis endangers the dominion he has over our mind.

In the moment of the ego's battle, one has to appeal to a power that is superior to the mind. This is the fire of the Kundalini serpent of Hinduism.

Practice

With the practice, the experience or the direct living of any of the works that I have delivered to humanity, the practitioner will obviously achieve psychological emancipation.

There exist people who speak marvels about reincarnation, Atlantis, alchemy, the ego, astral projection, etc. However, they are experts on these matters only in the external world because they are only being informed intellectually. Deep down, these people do not know anything, and at the hour of death these expositors remain with nothing but knowledge stored in their memory. In the beyond, this does not serve any purpose because they continue with their consciousness asleep.

We have wasted our time miserably if we are imprisoned only in theories, if we have not carried out anything practical, if we have not become conscious about what I have taught in my books, or if we leave the teachings in the memory.

Memory is the formative principle of the Intellectual Center. When a person aspires for something more, looking through the limitations of his subconsciousness, seeing what he has deposited in his memory, analyzing and meditating upon the last occurrence or teachings of an esoteric book, only then will those values move to the emotional phase of the same Intellectual Center.

When one wants to know the deep meaning of certain teachings and surrenders in full to meditation, such teachings obviously move on to the Emotional Center and then they come to be felt in the depth of the soul.

When one has purely experienced these teachings (the cognizable values of the essence), then at last they remain deposited in the consciousness and are never again lost. The essence becomes enriched with the same cognizable values.

Now we comprehend the way to become conscious of the Gnostic teachings that I have delivered through my previously written books, as well as through this one.

Meditation is formidable in order to make us conscious of the Gnostic teachings, but let us not commit the error of leaving the teachings exclusively in theories or in the memory. If we proceed in this manner we will never achieve the dominion of the mind.

The Requisite

The crude reality of facts demonstrates to us that many are those who have not comprehended the transcendence of the Gnostic esoteric work, and that great majorities are not good heads of households.

When one is not a good head of household, it is clear that one is not prepared to enter onto the path of the razor's edge. In order to work on the revolution of the dialectic, one needs to have reached the level of being a good head of household.

A fanatic, lunatic, whimsical type of person, etc., cannot be good for an integral revolution. A subject who does not fulfill the duties of his home cannot achieve the great change. A person who is a bad father, a bad wife, a bad husband, or a person who abandons his home for whichever man or woman, will never be able to arrive at a radical transformation.

The cornerstone of revolutionary psychology requires that one has a perfect equilibrium at home by being a good spouse, a good parent, a good sibling, and a good child. One must have perfect completion of his duties that exist with this suffering humanity. One must convert himself into a decent person.

Whoever does not fulfill these requirements will never be able to advance in these revolutionary studies.

Defeatism

The intellectual animal, falsely called a human being, has the fixed idea that the total annihilation of the ego, the absolute dominion of sex and the inner Self-realization of the Being is something fantastic and impossible. However, he does not realize that this very subjective way of thinking is the fruit of defeatist psychological elements that manipulate the mind and the body of those people who have not awakened consciousness.

The people of this decrepit and degenerated era carry within their interior a psychic aggregate that is a great obstacle on the path of the annihilation of the ego: defeatism!

Defeatist thoughts handicap people from elevating their mechanical life to superior states. The majority of people consider themselves defeated even before beginning the struggle or the Gnostic esoteric work.

One has to observe and analyze oneself here and now, to discover within those facets that make up defeatism.

In synthesis, there exist three common defeatist attitudes:

1. To feel handicapped because of a lack of intellectual education.
2. To feel incapable of beginning the radical transformation.

3. To walk around with the psychological song, "I never have opportunities to change or to triumph!"

FIRST ATTITUDE:
FEELING HANDICAPPED BECAUSE OF A LACK OF EDUCATION

We have to remember that all of the great sages such as Hermes Trismegistus, Paracelsus, Plato, Socrates, Jesus the Christ, Homer, etc., never went to universities because verily, each person indeed has his own Master. This Master is the Being, who is beyond the mind and false rationalism. Therefore, do not confuse education with wisdom and knowledge.

The specific knowledge of the mysteries of life, cosmos, and nature is an extraordinary force that allows us to achieve integral revolution.

SECOND ATTITUDE:
FEELING INCAPABLE OF BEGINNING THE RADICAL TRANSFORMATION

The human-robots who are programmed by the Antichrist (materialistic science) feel that they are at a disadvantage because they do not feel capable enough. We must analyze the following: because of the influence of a false academic education that adulterates the values of the Being, the intellectual animal has created in his sensual mind two terrible "I's" that must be eliminated. The first is a fixed idea that states: "I am going to lose!" The second is a laziness to practice the Gnostic techniques through which we will acquire the knowledge that is needed to emancipate ourselves from all the mechanicity and to once and for all come out from this defeatist tendency.

THIRD ATTITUDE:
WALKING AROUND WITH THE PSYCHOLOGICAL SONG: "I NEVER HAVE OPPORTUNITIES TO CHANGE OR TO TRIUMPH!"

The thinking of the mechanical human being is: "Opportunities are never provided to me!" The scenes of existence can be modified and one creates his own circumstances.

Everything is the result of the Law of Action and Consequence. However, the possibility that a superior law transcends an inferior law exists.

The elimination of the "I" of defeatism is urgent and unpostponable. It is not the quantity of theories that matters, but the quantity of super-efforts that are exerted in the work of the revolution of the consciousness. The authentic human being fabricates, in the moment that he wishes, the opportune moments for his spiritual or psychological growth!

Psycho-astrology

It is written with fiery embers in the book of life that everyone who achieves the total elimination of the ego can change his astrological sign and its influences at will.

In the name of truth, I have to declare that the One who is within me has changed astrological signs at will.

The sign of my ex-personality was Pisces, but now I am Aquarius, a terrifically revolutionary sign!

We cannot deny the existence of the influences of the signs that manipulate us as long as the psychological revolution has not been carried out within us. But every student on the path who aspires to enlightenment must begin by revolutionizing himself against that which the horoscopes establish.

That matter of one sign not being compatible with another sign is totally absurd because what are not compatible are the egos, those undesirable elements that we carry within.

The astrology of these times of the end is of no use or of any good because it is pure business. The authentic astrology of Chaldean sages has already been forgotten.

Machine-like people do not want to change because they say, "That is my sign, that is my zodiacal influence!" etc. I will never get tired of emphasizing that what is important is to change emotionally and mentally.

It is necessary to change mentally so that the authentic zodiacal forces that emanate from the Being in the Milky

Way may penetrate and become manifest in us, giving us a Permanent Center of Gravity.

We must not seek the light within horoscopes. The light surges forth when we have eliminated from within ourselves the Particular Characteristic Psychological Feature and when we have created a new flask—the mind—to pour into it the teachings of Psychoastrology (which I have taught in my book *Zodiacal Course*).

The Being and the Divine Mother are the only ones who can emancipate us from newspapers and cheap magazine horoscopes, thus giving us an integral education.

We have to shake off the dust of the centuries from ourselves and eliminate all our rancid customs and beliefs and leave astrological fanaticism behind, things such as, "It is my zodiacal influence. I can't help it. What can I do?" Such a subjective manner of thinking is a sophism of distraction of the ego.

The Rhetoric of the Ego

By analyzing the three-brained biped called a human being, we arrive at the logical conclusion that he does not yet have a Permanent Center of Consciousness, a Permanent Center of Gravity.

We cannot affirm that human bipeds are individualized; we are sure that they are only instinctualized. In other words, they are only impelled by "I's" that manipulate the Instinctive Center at their pleasure.

The beloved ego does not have any individuality. The ego is merely a sum of conflicted factors, a sum of small loose cathexis of egotistical psychic energies.

Each small "I" of those that constitute the legion called ego really has its own personal criteria, its own projects, its own ideas and its own rhetoric.

The rhetoric of the ego is the art of speaking well, with elegance, in such a subtle way that we do not realize at which moment we have fallen into error. The rhetoric of the ego is so subliminal that our consciousness sleeps without us ever realizing it.

We see the ego with its rhetoric leading countries on an arms race: "The volume of heavy commerce among the Third World countries duplicated between 1973 and 1976 [airplanes, warships, and armored transport], while their imports doubled." The interesting thing is that in an age in which they talk about arms control and peace, the countries in the process of supposed "development" with the help of the supposedly "industrialized" ones, increase their capacity for destruction! Is this truly the appropriate road for disarmament and world peace? On the contrary, it is the rhetoric of the ego.

While human bipeds continue to be fascinated with inventions and with all the apparent marvels of the Antichrist [materialistic science], in Ethiopia hundreds of thousands of people have died of hunger since 1973. Is this civilization? This is the rhetoric of the ego...

The human biped only wants to live in his tiny world, which is no longer good for anything. Materialistic psychology (experimental psychology) is good for nothing. Proof of this is the fact that materialistic psychology has not been able to solve the mental problems that affect the country of the United States. For example, in the large cities of the American Union, the famous "gangs" continue to multiply. Let us take a look at New York City where many "Pool Sharks" exist. They are a group of people whose members are about 30 years old and wear dirty clothes and leather boots. They meet on roof tops and pride themselves on being good billiard players. "The Unknown Cyclists" are also more or less the same age. They dress in the fashion of the "Hell's Angels" and wear leather jackets with big zippers. Their bicycles are old Schwinns that have been adapted with elongated forks to resemble motorcycles.

Violence is an accepted part of the lives of each of the thousands of members of gangs that exist in that country. Painfully enough, there are human bipeds of other countries who want to imitate them. Is this psychological liberation? False! This is the rhetoric of the ego, which has deceived everyone. It is only by living and putting into practice the teachings that I have delivered in this entire authentic treatise of revolutionary psychology that human bipeds will be able to free themselves from the rhetoric of the ego.

The Permanent Center of Consciousness

Three-brained bipeds do not have any individuality; they do not have a Permanent Center of Consciousness (PCC). Each of their thoughts, feelings and actions depends upon the calamity of the "I" that controls the capital centers of the human machine at a specific moment.

We, the ones who through many years of pain and sacrifice have struggled and fought for the Gnostic Movement, have practically observed unpleasant things. Many neophytes, with tears in their eyes, swore to work for Gnosis until the end of their days. They promised eternal fidelity to the Great Cause and delivered tremendous speeches. But what happened? What became of their tears of blood? What became of their great oaths? Everything was useless... It was only a fleeting "I" that had sworn fidelity. But, all of a sudden another "I" replaced that "I" and the individual wound up withdrawing from Gnosis, betraying the Great Cause, or enrolling themselves in other petty schools—in the end, betraying the Gnostic Institutions.

Really, the human being cannot have continuity of purpose because he does not have the PCC, he is not an individual, and he has an "I" that is a sum of many small "I's."

Many are those who await the eternal beatitude with the death of the physical body. However, the death of the body does not resolve the problem of the "I."

After death, the loose cathexis (the ego) continues enveloped in its molecular body. So the body of the human biped dies, but the loose cathexis (the energy of the ego) inside its molecular body continues. Later, this ego perpetuates itself in our descendants, returning to satisfy its desires and continuing to act out its same tragedies.

The hour has arrived to comprehend the necessity of producing within us a definite integral revolution in order to establish the PCC, a Permanent Center of Consciousness. Only in this way can we individualize ourselves; only in this way can we cease being a legion; only in this way can we become cognizant individuals.

The human being of today is similar to a ship full of many passengers, each passenger having his own plans and projects. The human being of today does not have a single mind; instead he has many minds. Each "I" has its own mind.

Fortunately, within the human biped there exists something else, the Essence. Reflecting seriously on such a principle, we can conclude that this is the most elevated psychic material with which we can give shape to our Soul.

We create Soul by awakening this Essence. To awaken the Essence is to awaken consciousness. To awaken consciousness is the equivalent of creating within us a PCC. Only the one who awakens consciousness can become an individual. However, the individual is not the goal because later we have to achieve super-individuality.

Super-individuality

We need to de-egotize ourselves in order to individualize ourselves, and then super-individualize ourselves. We need to dissolve the "I" in order to have the PCC (which we had studied about in the previous chapter).

The pluralized "I" foolishly wastes the psychic material in atomic explosions of anger, covetousness, lust, envy, pride, laziness, gluttony, etc.

Once the "I" is dead, the psychic material accumulates within us and thus, becomes the PCC.

In this day and age, the human being, or better said, the biped who classifies himself as "human," is really a machine that is controlled by the legion of the "I."

Let us observe the tragedy of people in love: how many promises they make! How many tears they shed! How many good intentions they state! But, what happens? All that is left are their sad memories. They marry, then time transpires, and the husband falls in love with another woman or the wife falls in love with another man, and their castle in the sky falls to the ground. Why? It is because the person does not yet have his PCC.

The small "I" that swore eternal love is replaced by another small "I" that has nothing to do with that promise. That is all. We need to become individuals and this is only possible by creating a PCC.

We need to create a PCC and this is only possible by dissolving the pluralized "I."

All of the inner contradictions of the human being, if seen in a mirror, would be enough to drive anyone insane. The source of such contradictions is the plurality of the "I."

Whosoever wants to dissolve the "I" has to begin by knowing his inner contradictions. Unfortunately, people like to deceive themselves in order not to see their own contradictions.

Whosoever wants to dissolve the "I" has to begin by not being a liar. All people are liars unto themselves; everyone lies to himself.

If we want to know the plurality of the "I" and our perennial contradictions, we must then not deceive ourselves. People deceive themselves so as not to see their internal contradictions.

With just reason, everyone who discovers his intimate contradictions feels ashamed of himself. He comprehends that he is a nobody, that he is a wretched person, a miserable worm of the earth.

To discover our own intimate contradictions is a success because then our inner judgment is liberated spontaneously, thus permitting us to see with clarity the path of individuality and that of super-individuality.

1. Integral Well-being

We need integral well-being. We all suffer, we have bitterness in our life, and we want to change.

In any case, I think that integral well-being is the result of self-respect. This would seem quite strange to an economist, or to a theosophist, etc. What could self-respect have to do with economic matters, with problems related with labor or with the labor force, with capital, etc.?

I want to comment about how our level of Being attracts our life... We used to live in a very beautiful house in Mexico City. Behind that house there was a very large lot of land that was empty. One ordinary day, a group of "parachutists" (a term used in Mexico to name those people who come to land on large lots of sparsely settled areas) invaded that land. Soon they built their cardboard huts and established themselves there. Unquestionably, they became something dirty in that colony. I do not want to underestimate them, but if their cardboard huts were kept clean, I would not object to them. Unfortunately, a frightening lack of hygiene existed among those people.

I observed the life of those people very carefully from the roof of my house: they insulted each other, they hurt each other, they did not respect their fellowmen; in synthesis, their life was horrifying, with miseries and abominations.

Police patrol cars were never seen there before; now the police were always visiting the colony. Before, that colony was peaceful; afterwards, it became an inferno. Thus, in this manner I was able to verify that the level of Being attracts our life, obviously.

Let us suppose that one of those inhabitants resolved from one day to the next to respect himself and to respect others; obviously, he would change.

What is understood by respecting oneself? To abandon delinquency, to not steal, to not fornicate, to not commit adultery, to not envy the well-being of one's fellowman, to be humble and simple, to abandon laziness and become an active, clean, decent person, etc.

Upon respecting himself, a citizen changes his level of Being and upon changing his level of Being, he unquestionably attracts new circumstances. Thus, he will relate with more decent people, with different people, and possibly, those types of relations will provoke an economic and social change in his existence. What I said about integral self-respect provoking an economic well-being has been fulfilled. But if one does not know how to respect oneself, one will also not respect his fellowmen and will condemn oneself to a wretched and unhappy life.

The beginning of integral well-being is self-respect.

2. Self-reflection

Let us not forget that the exterior is merely the reflection of the interior; this has already been stated by Immanuel Kant, the philosopher of Konigsberg. If we carefully study the *Critique of Pure Reasoning*, we certainly discover that the "exterior is the interior" (textual words of one of the great thinkers of all times).

The exterior image of a human being and the circumstances that surround him are the outcome of his self-image; these words "self" and "image" are profoundly significant.

Precisely in these moments, the photograph of James comes into my memory. Somebody took a photograph of our friend James and something interesting happened; in the photograph there appears to be two James: one that is very still, in a position of attention, with the face looking forward; the other appeared to be walking in front of him with the face in a different position. How is it possible that two James appear in one photograph?

I think that it is worthwhile to enlarge that photograph, because it might help us in order to show it to all the people who become interested in these studies. Obviously, I think that the second James would be the self-reflection of the first James; for it is written that the exterior image of a person and the circumstances that surround him are the outcome of his self-image.

It is also written that the exterior is merely the reflection of the interior. So, if we do not respect ourselves, if the interior image of ourselves is very mediocre, if we are full of psychological defects, of moral scum, unquestionably, unpleasant events will surge forth in the exterior world, such as economic and social difficulties, etc. Let us not forget that the exterior image of a person and the circumstances that surround him are the outcome of his self-image.

We all have a self-image. Outside of us exists the physical image that can be photographed; however, inside of us we have another image that cannot. To clarify this better, we will state that outside we have the physical and perceptible image and inside we have that image of a psychological and hypersensible type.

If on the outside we have a wretched and miserable image and if this image is accompanied by unpleasant circumstances, like a difficult economic situation, problems of all types, conflicts, whether at home, at work, or on the street, etc., this happens simply because our psychological image is wretched, defective and horrifying. Thus, we reflect our misery, our nothingness, that which we think we are, onto our environment.

If we want to change, we need to make a total and great change. Image, values, and identity must change radically.

In several of my books I have stated that each of us is a mathematical point in space that agrees to serve as a vehicle to a specific sum of values. Some serve as vehicles of wise values and others serve as vehicles of mediocre values. That is why each person is a different person. The majority of human beings serve as vehicles for the values of the ego, the "I." These values can be positive or negative. Therefore, image, values, and identity are a single whole.

I stated that we must undergo a total transformation. Therefore, emphatically I affirm that identity, values, and image must be totally changed.

We need a new identity, new values and a new image. This is a psychological revolution, an inner revolution. It is absurd to continue within this vicious circle in which we presently move. We need to change integrally.

The self-image of a person originates his exterior image. For the term self-image, I allude to the psychological image that we have within. What could our psychological image be? Could it be that of the irate, of the covetous, of the lustful, of the envious, of the proud, of the lazy, of the glutton, or what? Wherever the image that we have of ourselves may be, or better said, whichever our self-image would be, this interior image will originate, as is usual, the exterior image.

The exterior image of someone, even if it is well dressed, could be that of someone needy. Is the image of the arrogant one, of the one who has become obnoxious, that does not have a grain of humility, perhaps a beautiful image? How does a lustful person behave; how does he live; what aspect does his bedroom present; what is his behavior in his or her intimate life with the opposite sex; perhaps he or she is already degenerated? What could be the external image of an envious person, of someone who suffers because of his fellowman's well-being and who in secrecy harms others out of envy? What is the image of a lazy person who does not want to work and is dirty and abominable? And what is the image of a glutton...?

Therefore, the exterior image is indeed the outcome of the interior image. This is irrefutable.

If a person learns to respect himself, his life will then change, not only within the field of ethics or that of psychology, but also within the social, economic and even political fields. But this person has to change. That is why I insist that identity, values, and image must be changed.

The present identity, values, and image that we have of ourselves are miserable. This is the cause of why our present social life is full of conflicts and economic problems. In this day and age, nobody is happy; nobody is joyful. Therefore, can the image, values, and identity that we have be changed? Can we acquire a new identity, new values, and a new image? I definitely affirm that it is possible.

Unquestionably, we need to disintegrate the ego. We all have an "I." When we knock at a door we are asked, who is it? We answer: "It's me." But, who is that me? Who is that myself?

Verily, the ego is indeed a sum of negative and positive values. We must disintegrate the ego, put an end to those positive and negative values. Then we can serve as a vehicle for new values, the values of the Being. Consequently, if we want to eliminate all the values that we presently have in order to provoke a change, we need a new didactic.

3. Psychoanalysis

There exists a didactic that teaches us how to know and how to eliminate the positive and negative values that we carry within. This didactic is called inner psychoanalysis.

In order to know our psychological defects it is necessary to appeal to inner psychoanalysis. A great difficulty arises when we appeal to inner psychoanalysis; I want to emphatically refer to the force of counter-transference (which is this great difficulty).

We can investigate ourselves, we can introvert ourselves, but when we attempt to, the difficulty of counter-transference emerges. The solution to this difficulty lies in knowing how to transfer our attention inward, with the purpose of exploring ourselves in order to know ourselves and to eliminate the negative values that harm us psychologically, socially, economically, politically, and even spiritually.

Unfortunately, I repeat, when one tries to introvert oneself in order to explore oneself and to know oneself, counter-transference immediately arises.

So counter-transference is a force that makes introversion difficult. If counter-transference did not exist, then introversion would be easier.

We need inner psychoanalysis; we need intimate self-investigation in order to really know ourselves. HOMO NOSCE TE IPSUM. *Man, know thyself, thus thou shalt know the Universe and the Gods.*

When one knows oneself, one can change. For as long as one does not know oneself, any change will become subjective. However, before anything else, we need self-analysis. How can the force of counter-transference (which makes intimate psychoanalysis or self-psychoanalysis difficult) be overcome? This can only be possible by means of transactional analysis and structural analysis.

When one appeals to structural analysis, one then knows those psychological structures that make intimate introspection difficult and impossible. Thus, when we know such psychological structures we comprehend them, and by comprehending them we overcome the obstacle.

But we need something else, we also need transactional analysis. In the same manner that banks, and commercial transactions, etc., exist, so do psychological transactions.

The different psychic elements that we carry within our interior are subject to transactions, to exchanges, to struggles, to changes of position, etc. They are not something motionless; they always exist in a state of motion.

When one knows one's different psychological processes, one's different structures by means of transactional analysis, then the difficulties for psychological introspection concludes. Afterwards, the self-exploration of oneself is carried out with great success.

Whosoever achieves complete self-exploration of this or that defect, whether he explores himself in order to know his anger, his covetousness, his lust, his laziness, his gluttony, etc., can carry out a formidable psychological progress.

In order to achieve complete self-exploration, one will have to first begin by segregating the defect that one wants to eliminate from oneself in order for it to be subsequently dissolved.

A percentage of psychic Essence is liberated when a defect is disintegrated. Thus, the psychic Essence that is bottled up within our defects will be completely liberated when we disintegrate each and every one of our false values, in other words, our defects. Thus, the radical transformation of ourselves will occur when the totality of our Essence is liberated. Then, in that precise moment, the eternal values of the Being will express themselves through us. Unquestionably, this would be marvelous not only for us, but also for all of humanity.

When we achieve the total disintegration or annihilation of our negative values, we will respect ourselves and others. Thus, we will become, we might say, a fountain of kindness for the entire world, a perfect, conscious and marvelous creature.

Therefore, the mystical self-image of an awakened person will consequently or as a corollary originate the perfect image of a noble citizen. His circumstances will also be beneficial in every sense. He will be a golden link in the great universal chain of life. He will be an example for the entire world, a fountain of joy for many beings, an enlightened one in the most transcendental sense of the word, someone who will enjoy continuous and delightful ecstasy.

4. Mental Dynamics

In mental dynamics we need to know how and why the mind functions as it does.

Unquestionably, the mind is an instrument that we must learn to use consciously. But it would be absurd for such an instrument to be efficient for us if we first did not know the how and why of the mind.

When one knows the how and the why of the mind, when one knows the different functionalisms of the mind, then one can control it. Thus, the mind becomes a useful and perfect instrument through which we can work for the benefit of humanity.

Truly, we need a realistic system if we want to know the full potential of the human mind.

In this day and age many systems for the control of the mind exist abundantly. There exist people who think that certain artificial exercises can be magnificent for the control of their minds. Schools exist; theories about the mind are abundant; many systems exist, but how would it be possible to make something useful of the mind? Let us reflect that if we do not know the many how and the whys of the mind, we will never be able to perfect it.

We need to know the different functionalisms of the mind if we want it to be perfect. How does it function? Why does it function? Those how and whys are definitive.

If, for example, we throw a stone into a lake, we will see that waves are formed. These are the reactions of the lake, of the water, against the stone. Similarly, if someone says something ironic, such a statement reaches the mind and the mind reacts against it; conflicts then subsequently arise.

The entire world is in turmoil; the entire world lives in conflicts. I have carefully observed the debate panels of many organizations, schools, etc.; they do not respect each other. Why? It is because they do not respect themselves.

Observe a senate, a chamber of representatives or simply a school board: if someone says something, another feels alluded to, and becomes angry and says something even worse, then they quarrel amongst themselves and the members of the board of directors end up in a great chaos. This reaction of the minds of those people against the impacts of the exterior world is very serious.

One has to truly appeal to introspective psychoanalysis to explore one's own mind. It is necessary to know ourselves a little more within the intellectual sphere. For example, why do we react upon hearing the words of a fellowman? In these conditions we are always victims... If someone wants us to be content, it is enough for that person to give us a few pats on the back and tell us a few amiable words. If someone wants to see us upset, it would be enough for them to tell us a few unpleasant words.

Therefore, where is our true intellectual freedom? Where is it? We concretely depend on others; we are slaves. Our psychological processes depend exclusively upon other people; we do not rule over our own psychological processes and this is terrible.

Others are the ones who rule us and our intimate processes. For instance: all of a sudden a friend comes and invites us to a party. We go to our friend's house and he gives us a drink. We accept it out of courtesy and we drink it, however another drink follows and we also drink that one, then another, and another until we end up drunk. Thus, our friend was the lord and master of our psychological process.

Could a mind like that be good for anything? If someone rules us, if the entire world has the right to rule us, then where is our intellectual freedom? Where is it? Suddenly, we are with a person of the opposite sex and we become very identified with that person; we end up in fornication and adultery. Conclusion, that person of the opposite sex had the upper hand and overcame our psychological processes; that person controlled us, subjected us to his or her own will. Is this freedom?

Verily, the intellectual animal, falsely called a human being, has indeed been educated to deny his identity, values, and image. Where is the authentic identity, values, and intimate image of each one of us? Is it perhaps the ego or the personality? No! By means of introspective psychoanalysis we can go beyond the ego and discover the Being.

Unquestionably, the Being is in himself our authentic identity, values and image. The Being is in himself the K-H, the Kosmos Human or Human Kosmos. Unfortunately, as I have already stated, the intellectual animal, falsely called a human being, has educated himself in order to deny his inner values, has fallen into the materialism of this degenerated era. Hence, he has surrendered himself to all the vices of the Earth and treads upon the path of error.

To accept this present negative culture subjectively (inspired in our interior) by following the path of least resistance is an error. Unfortunately, people in this day and age enjoys following the path of least resistance and accept the false materialistic culture of these times; they allow it to become installed in their psyche and this is how they arrive at the denial of the true values of their Being.

5. The Laconic Action of the Being

The laconic action of the Being is the concise manifestation, the brief action, which in synthesis the real Being of each one of us executes. This action is mathematical and exact, like a Pythagorean table.

I want you to reflect very well upon the laconic action of the Being. Remember that above, within the infinite starry space, every action is the result of an equation and of an exact formula. Likewise, as a logical deduction, we must emphatically affirm that our true image, the inner Kosmic Human, is beyond false values. He is perfect.

Unquestionably, each action of the Being is the result of an equation and of an exact formula.

There have been cases in which the Being has succeeded in expressing himself through someone who has achieved a change of image, values, and identity. Thus, that one has in fact become a prophet, an enlightened one.

However, there have also been lamentable cases of people who have served as vehicles of their own Being and have not comprehended the intentions of the divine.

When someone serves as a vehicle of his Being and does not work disinterestedly in favor of humanity, he has not understood what an equation and an exact formula of every laconic action of the Being is. Only the one who renounces the fruits of action, who does not expect any reward whatsoever, who is only motivated by love in order to work, in favor of his fellowmen, has certainly comprehended the laconic action of the Being.

I repeat, we need to undergo a total change of ourselves. Image, values, and identity must change. How beautiful it is to have the image of a young terrestrial man, but what is even better is to have the spiritual and heavenly image here and now, in the flesh and bones.

Instead of possessing the negative values of the ego, we should have the positive values of the Being within our hearts and within our minds.

Commonly our identity is vulgar, yet in order to stop being vulgar, we must put our identity at the service of the Being.

Let us reflect on the necessity of becoming the living expression of the Being...

The Being is the Being and the reason for the Being to be, is to be the Being itself. Let us clearly distinguish between what expression is and what self-expression is. The ego can express itself but it will never have self-expression. The ego expresses itself through the personality and its expressions are subjective; it says what others said, it narrates what others narrated, it explains what others explained, but it does not have the evident self-expression of the Being.

The real objective self-expression of the Being is what matters. When the Being expresses himself through us, he does it in a perfect and laconic way.

We have to disintegrate the ego on the basis of inner psychoanalysis in order for the Verb, the Word of the Being, to be expressed through us.

Self-esteem

Much is said about feminine vanity. Truly, vanity is the living manifestation of self-esteem.

The woman before a mirror adoring herself, worshipping herself with frenzy, is a complete narcissist. The woman adorns herself the best way she can, she paints herself, she curls her hair, etc. She purposely does this so that others will say, "You are gorgeous, you are beautiful, you are divine, etc."

The "I" always enjoys the admiration of others; this is why it adorns itself. The "I" believes itself to be beautiful, pure, ineffable, holy, virtuous, etc. No one believes himself to be evil; all people consider themselves good and just.

Self-esteem is something terrible. For example, the fanatics of materialism do not accept the superior dimensions of space due to their self-esteem. They love themselves too much, and as usual they demand that the superior dimensions of space, of the cosmos and of all ultra-sensible life, must subject themselves to their personal whims. They are not capable of going beyond their narrow criteria and theories, beyond their beloved ego and their mental precepts.

Physical death does not resolve the fatal problem of the ego. Only the psychological death of the "I" can resolve the problem of human pain. However, the "I" loves itself too much and does not want to die whatsoever. As long as the "I" exists, the wheel of Samsara (the fatal wheel of human tragedy) will turn.

When we are really in love we renounce the "I." In life it is very rare to find someone who is really in love. Everyone is impassioned and this is not love. People become impassioned when they meet someone they like. They discover that the other person has the same errors, qualities and defects and this serves as a mirror for them to contemplate themselves totally. Indeed, they are not in love with the loved one, they are only in love with themselves. They enjoy seeing themselves in the mirror (their loved one). This is how they meet and then suppose that they are in love. The "I" enjoys seeing itself before the mirror or feels happy seeing itself within the person that has its same qualities, virtues and defects.

Preachers speak much about the truth, but is it possible to know the truth when self-esteem exists within ourselves?

Only by ridding ourselves of self-esteem, only by having the mind free of assumptions, can we experience, in the absence of the "I," that which is the truth.

Many will criticize this book *The Revolution of the Dialectic*. As usual, pseudo-sapient people will laugh at these revolutionary statements because these teachings are a crime for them due to the fact that they do not coincide with their "mental assumptions" and complicated theories that they have in their memories.

Erudite persons are not capable of listening to revolutionary psychology with a spontaneous mind, free of mental assumptions, theories, preconceptions, etc. They are not capable of opening themselves up to what is new with an integral mind, with a mind that is not divided up by the battle of the antitheses.

Erudite people only listen in order to compare with the assumptions stored in their memory. Erudite people only listen to translate according to their own language of prejudices and preconceptions and to arrive at the conclusion that the teachings of the revolution of the dialectic are fantasies. This is how erudite persons always are. Their minds are already so degenerated that they are not capable of discovering anything new.

The erudite "I," with its arrogance, wants everything to coincide with its theories and mental assumptions. The erudite "I" wants all its whims to be fulfilled and it wants the cosmos in its totality to be submitted to its laboratory experiments.

The ego despises everyone who hurts its self-esteem. The ego adores its theories and preconceptions.

Many times we despise someone without any reason. Why? Simply, because that person personifies some errors that we carry well hidden within and we do not like that person exhibiting them. In fact, deep within us, we carry the errors that we blame others for.

No one is perfect in this world; we are all made out of the same mold. Each one of us is nothing more than a slug within the bosom of the Great Reality.

The one who does not have a defect in a specific area has it in another area. Some do not covet money but they covet fame, honors, love affairs, etc. Others do not commit adultery with someone else's spouse but they enjoy altering doctrines, mixing creeds in the name of universal fraternity.

Some are not jealous of their spouse but they are jealous of friendships, creeds, sects, things, etc. This is how we human beings are, always made out of the same mold. There does not exist a person who does not adore himself. We have listened to individuals who enjoy talking about themselves for hours and hours, about their marvels, their talents, their virtues, etc.

The ego loves itself so much that it envies others' well-being. Women adorn themselves with many things, partly out of vanity and partly to awaken envy in other women. They all envy each other. They all envy the other's dress, the beautiful necklace, etc. They all adore themselves and do not want to see themselves as less than the others. They are one hundred percent narcissistic.

Some pseudo-occultists or brethren from many sects adore themselves so much that they have begun to believe themselves to be mountains of humility and sanctity. They feel proud of their own humility. They are terribly arrogant.

There is not a pseudo-occultist, younger brother or sister who deep within does not presume sanctity, splendor, and spiritual beauty.

No pseudo-occultist brothers or sisters believe themselves to be evil or perverse; they all presume to be saints, perfect even when not only are they evil, but perverse as well.

The beloved ego adores itself too much and presumes, even when it does not say it, of being good and perfect.

Ahimsa: Nonviolence

Ahimsa, nonviolence, is the pure thought of India; ahimsa is indeed inspired by universal love. The word *himsa* means "to want to kill; to want to harm." Therefore, *ahimsa* is the renunciation of all death or harm caused by violence or even such intentions.

Ahimsa is the opposite of egotism; it is absolute altruism and love; it is upright action. Mahatma Gandhi made of ahimsa the wand of his political doctrine.

Gandhi defined the manifestation of ahimsa in the following manner:

> "Nonviolence does not consist of renouncing all real struggles against evil. Nonviolence, as I conceive it, establishes a more active campaign against evil than the law of the Talion, whose nature itself results in the development of perversity. I raise before the immoral a mental opposition, and consequently, a moral one. I try to whet the tyrants sword, not by clashing it against better sharpened steel, but by disappointing his hopes by not offering any physical resistance. He will find in me a resistance of the soul that will escape his assault. This resistance will first of all blind him and will immediately force him to surrender. And the act of surrender will not humiliate the aggressor but will dignify him..."

There is not a more powerful weapon than a well directed mind!

The ego is the one that disunites, betrays, and establishes anarchy within this wretched suffering humanity. Egoism, treason, and the lack of brotherhood has divided humanity.

The "I" was not created by God, by the Spirit, or by matter. The "I" was created by our own mind and will cease to exist when we have comprehended it completely in all the levels of the mind. It is only through upright action, upright meditation, upright will, upright manner of earning a living, upright effort, and upright memory that we can dissolve the "I." If we

MAHATMA GANDHI

If one has... pride and egoism, there
is no nonviolence. Nonviolence is
impossible without humility. - Gandhi

truly want the revolution of the dialectic, it is urgent to comprehend all of this in depth.

The personality must not be confused with the "I." In fact, the personality is formed during the first seven years of childhood. The "I" is something different. It is the error that is perpetuated from century to century; it fortifies itself each time, more and more through the mechanics of recurrence.

The personality is energetic. It is born during infancy through habits, customs, ideas, etc., and it is fortified with the experiences of life. Therefore, both the personality as well as the "I" must be disintegrated. These psychological teachings are more revolutionary than those of Gurdjieff and Ouspensky.

The "I" utilizes the personality as an instrument of action. Thus, personalism is a mixture of ego and personality. Personality worship was invented by the "I." In fact, personalism engenders egoism, hatred, violence, etc. All of this is rejected by ahimsa.

Personality totally ruins esoteric organizations. Personality produces anarchy and confusion. Personalism can totally destroy any organization.

The ego fabricates a new personality each time it is reincorporated (returned to a new body). Therefore, each person is different in each new embodiment.

It is urgent to know how to live. When the "I" is dissolved, the Great Reality, true happiness, That which has no name, comes to us.

Let us distinguish between the Being and the "I." The human being of today only has the "I." The human being of today is an entity who is not yet complete. It is urgent to receive the Being; it is necessary to know that the Being is limitless happiness.

It is absurd to state that the Being is the "superior I," the "divine I," etc. The taste of the Being is much better than that of the ego, because the Being is universal and cosmic. Therefore, let us not try to make the "I" divine.

Ahimsa is nonviolence in thought, word and deed. Ahimsa is respect for others' ideas, respect for all religions, schools, sects, organizations, etc.

Let us not expect the "I" to evolve because the "I" never perfects itself. We need a total revolution of the consciousness. This is the only type of revolution that we accept.

The doctrine of ahimsa is based on the revolution of the dialectic, on the revolution of the consciousness.

As we die from moment to moment, harmony among human beings slowly begins to develop. As we die from moment to moment, the sense of cooperation replaces the sense of competition. As we die from moment to moment, little by little good will replaces evil will.

Human beings of good will accept ahimsa. It is impossible to initiate a new order in our psyche while excluding the doctrine of nonviolence.

Ahimsa should be cultivated in homes by following the path of the perfect matrimony. It is only with nonviolence in thought and deed that happiness can reign in homes.

Ahimsa should be the foundation of daily living, at the office, in the factory, in the countryside, at home, on the street, etc. We should live the doctrine of nonviolence.

Gregarious Conduct

Gregarious conduct is a tendency that the human machine allows. This tendency is to ally itself with other human machines without distinction or control of any type.

Let us examine what one does when in a group or in a crowd. I am sure that very few people would dare go out into the street and throw stones at someone. However, when in a group, they do so. Someone can slip into a public demonstration and become fired up with enthusiasm; thus, they end up joining the masses in throwing stones. Although, later he will ask himself, why did I do that?

The human being behaves very differently when he is in a crowd. He does things that he would not normally do when he is alone. Why does this happen? This occurs because he opens the doors (his senses) to negative impressions and he ends up doing things that he would never do if he were alone.

When one opens the doors to negative impressions, one not only alters the order of the emotional center which is in the heart, but moreover one makes this center negative. For example, if somebody we know is filled with anger because another person hurt him, we open our doors to those impressions and end up taking the side of our friend and feeling animosity towards the one who hurt him. We too become filled with anger, without even having played a part in the matter.

Let us suppose that one opens the doors to a negative impression of a drunkard; one then ends up accepting a drink, then another, and another, and so forth. In conclusion, one ends up being a drunkard too.

Let us suppose that one opens the doors to the negative impressions of a person of the opposite sex; most likely, one ends up fornicating and committing all types of transgressions.

If we open the doors to the negative impressions of a drug addict, then maybe we will end up smoking marijuana or consuming some type of intoxicants. As a conclusion, failure will come.

Thus, this is the way that human beings infect each other within their negative atmospheres. Thieves alter other people into becoming thieves. Murderers infect someone else. Drug addicts infect other people. This is how drug addicts, thieves, usurers, murderers, etc., multiply. Why? Because we commit the error of always opening our doors to negative emotions and this is never right. Therefore, let us select our emotions.

If someone brings us positive emotions of light, beauty, harmony, happiness, love, and perfection, then let us open the doors of our heart to him. But if someone brings us negative emotions of hate, violence, jealousy, drugs, alcohol, fornication and adultery, why should we open the doors of our heart to him? Let us close them! Close the doors to all negative emotions.

When one reflects on gregarious conduct, one can modify it perfectly and make something better out of life.

Deformation of the Word

The explosion of a cannon destroys the glass of a window. On the other hand, a soft word pacifies anger or wrath. Nevertheless, an insulting, inharmonious word produces anger or melancholy, sadness, hatred, etc.

It is said that silence is golden, but it is better stated with the following words: it is as incorrect to speak when one must be silent as it is to be silent when one must speak!

There are criminal silences, there are infamous words. One must calculate with nobility of manner the result of spoken words, for often times one hurts others with words in an unconscious manner.

Words filled with a sense of bad intentions produce fornication in the world of the mind. Arhythmic words (distorted words) engender violence in the world of the cosmic mind.

One must never condemn anyone with the verb because one must never judge anyone. Slander, gossip, and calumny have filled the world with pain and bitterness.

If we work with Sexual Super-dynamics, we have to comprehend that the creative energies are exposed to all kinds of modifications. These energies of the libido can be modified into powers of light or darkness; it all depends on the quality of the words.

The perfect human being speaks words of perfection. The Gnostic student who wishes to follow the path of the revolution of the dialectic must become accustomed to controlling the tongue. One must learn how to handle the word.

It is not what enters the mouth that causes harm to humans, but rather what comes out of it! The mouth supplies insults, intrigues, defamation, calumny, and debates. All of these things are what harms humans.

Therefore, avoid all types of fanaticism because we cause great harm to human beings, to our fellow men, with it. One not only hurts others with insulting words or with fine and artistic ironies, but also with the tone of the voice, with the inharmonious and arhythmic accent.

Knowing How to Listen

We have to learn how to listen. In order to learn how to listen, we have to awaken the consciousness.

In order to learn how to listen one has to know how to be present because the one who is listening is always escaping into his own psychological country or city.

The human personality and the physical body (because it is its vehicle) do not know how to listen.

People are filled with themselves, with their pride, with their faculties, and with their theories.

Therefore, there does not exist even a little corner or empty space within for knowledge, for the word. We must have our bowl facing upwards, like the Buddha, in order to receive the Christic word.

Psychological listening is very difficult. We have to learn to be attentive in order to know how to listen. We have to become more receptive to the word.

People do not remember their previous existences because they are not in their psychological house, they are outside of it.

One has to remember oneself. One has to relax the body as many times as one can during the day.

People commit many errors because they forget their Being. Great things happen when one remembers the Self.

Consultation is necessary but the important thing is to know how to listen. In order to know how to listen, one has to have the emotional, motor, and intellectual centers in supreme attention.

False education impedes one from listening. False education harms the five centers of the human machine—the intellectual, motor, emotional, instinctive, and sexual centers.

One has to listen with a spontaneous mind, free of mental assumptions, theories, and preconceptions. One has to open oneself to what is new with an integral mind, with the mind not divided by the battle of antitheses.

The Exactness of the Term

As the basis of his dialectic, Socrates demanded precision of terminology. In our revolution of the dialectic, we demand precision of the verb as a foundation.

The word is a distinctive human feature; it is the instrument of individual expression and communication among humans. It is the vehicle of exterior language and the discharge or exteriorization of the complicated interior language, which can be utilized by both the Being or the ego.

Plato, in the dialogue *Phaedo*, expressed to one of his disciples a concept that is famous for its profundity, moral delicacy, and as a human principle of idiomatic propriety. It states the following:

> "Be it known unto you, my dear Crito, that speaking in an improper manner is not only committing a fault in what is said, but also a type of damage that is caused to the souls."

If we want to resolve problems, we must abstain from expressing our opinion. Every opinion can be debated. We must resolve a problem by meditating upon it. It is necessary to resolve it with the mind and the heart. We must learn to think for ourselves. To repeat like parrots the opinions of others is absurd.

When the ego is annihilated, the mind's processing of options disappears. An opinion is the emission of a concept out of fear that another concept might be the truth, and this indicates ignorance.

It is urgent to learn not to identify with problems. It is necessary to explore ourselves sincerely and then maintain mental and verbal silence.

The Psychological Robot

The intellectual animal is similar to a robot programmed by mechanical wheels; he is also similar to a clock because he keeps repeating the same movements of his past existences.

The intellectual animal, falsely called a human being, is a psychological robot who does nothing; everything just happens to him. The Being is the only one who does anything. The Being causes to surge forth what he wants because he is not a mechanical entity.

One has to cease being an intellectual robot because a robot always repeats the same thing; he does not have any independence.

The psychological robot is influenced by the laws of the Moon: recurrence, conception, death, hatred, egoism, violence, conceit, haughtiness, self-importance, immoderate covetousness, etc.

One has to work with super-dynamics in order to create a Permanent Center of Gravity and become independent of the Moon.

In order to cease being a psychological robot, it becomes necessary to dominate oneself. Faust achieved it, but Cornelius Agrippa did not achieve it because he just chose to theorize.

People are interested in exploiting the world, but what is more important is to exploit oneself, because the one who exploits himself dominates the world.

The psychological robot who wants to become a Man and then a Superman must develop the capacity of sustaining the notes. When someone really wants to cease being a machine, he has to undergo the first crisis: Mi-Fa, and then undergo the second crisis: La-Si.

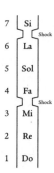

The key of the triumphant ones (in order to pass the crisis and to cease being a psychological robot) is: choice, change, and decision. The entire work is done in seven scales; afterwards, one acquires the Nirionissian sound of the universe.

Anger

Anger annihilates the capacity to think and to resolve the problems it originates. Obviously, anger is a negative emotion.

Two negative emotions of anger that confront each other do not achieve peace or creative comprehension.

Unquestionably, when we project anger onto another human being, a crumbling of our own image is always produced; this is never convenient in the world of interrelations.

The diverse processes of anger lead the human being towards horrible social, economic, and psychological failures. It is clear that one's health is also affected by anger.

There exist certain foolish persons who enjoy anger since it gives them a certain air of superiority. In these cases, anger is combined with pride.

Anger is also usually combined with conceit and even with self-sufficiency. Kindness is a much more crushing force than anger.

An angry argument is nothing but excitement lacking conviction. On confronting anger, we should decide, we should choose, the type of emotion that is most convenient to us.

Whosoever lets himself be controlled by anger destroys his own image. The person who has complete self-control will always be on top.

Frustration, fear, doubt, and guilt originate the processes of anger; they cause anger. Whosoever liberates himself from these four negative emotions will dominate the world. To accept negative passions is something that goes against self-respect.

Anger belongs to crazy people; it serves no purpose; it leads us to violence. The goal of violence is to lead us to violence, and this produces more violence.

The Personality

The personality is multiple and has many hidden depths. The karma of previous existences is deposited into the personality. It is karma in the process of fulfillment or crystallization.

The impressions that are not digested become new psychic aggregates, and what is more serious, they become new personalities. The personality is not homogenous but rather heterogeneous and plural.

One must select impressions in the same manner that one chooses the things of life.

If one forgets oneself at a given instant, in a new event, new "I's" are formed, and if they are very strong they become new personalities within the personality. Therein lies the cause of many traumas, complexes, and psychological conflicts.

An impression that one does not digest may form into a personality within the personality, and if one does not accept it, it becomes a source of frightening conflicts.

Not all the personalities (which one carries within the personality) are accepted; the latter giving origin to many traumas, complexes, phobias, etc.

Before all else, it is necessary to comprehend the multiplicity of the personality. The personality is multiple in itself.

Therefore, there could be someone who may have disintegrated the psychic aggregates, but if he does not disintegrate the personality, he will not be able to attain authentic enlightenment and the joy of living.

When one knows oneself more and more, one knows others more.

The individual with an ego does not see things clearly and makes many mistakes. Even when tremendous logic exists in their analysis, those who have ego fail because they lack judgment.

If impressions are not digested, new "I's" are created. One has to learn to select impressions.

It is not a matter of "being better"; what interests us is change. The Being surges forth when one has changed and has ceased to exist.

The undesirable elements that we carry within our interior are the ones that control our perceptions, preventing us from having an integral perception, which brings us joy and happiness.

Cathexis

The psychic energy, cathexis, processing itself as an executive force, is formidable.

The reserves of intelligence are the different parts of the Being and are denominated as bound cathexis or psychic energy in a potential and static state.

The bound cathexis orients us in the work related with the disintegration of the ego and with the liberation of the mind.

The bound cathexis, contained within the mind, guides us in the work related with revolutionary psychology and with integral revolution.

The values of the Being constitute the bound cathexis.

Only the bound cathexis can liberate the mind through the disintegration of the undesirable psychic elements, which have been segregated by means of structural and transactional analysis.

Bound cathexis is different from loose cathexis, since the latter is the psychic energy that the ego utilizes to dominate the mind and the body for its manifestation.

We have to permit the bound cathexis (which is the dynamic psychic energy) to be the one to direct our existence.

We have to work psychologically in order for the bound cathexis to enter into activity to dominate and govern the free cathexis. This free cathexis is the energy of the body that has always been pitifully dominated by the loose cathexis, which is the ego.

Mystical Death

We have suffered much with the members of the Gnostic Movement. Many have sworn fidelity in front of the altar of the sanctuaries; many have solemnly promised to work in the Great Work until total Self-realization; many are those who have cried swearing to never ever withdraw from the Gnostic Movement; however, it is painful to say, everything has been in vain. Almost everyone fled; they became enemies, blaspheming, fornicating, committing adultery, and went onto the black path. Really, the human being's terrible contradictions are due to him having a fatal foundation and a tragic basis; the said foundation is the plurality of the "I," the plurality of the loose cathexis that we all carry within.

It is urgent to know that the "I" is a mass of psychic energies, of loose cathexes, which reproduce in the lower animal depths of the human being. Each loose cathexis is a small "I" that enjoys certain auto-independence.

These "I's," these loose cathexes, struggle amongst themselves. "I should read a newspaper," says the intellectual "I." "I will ride a bicycle," argues the motor "I," "I am hungry," declares the "I" of digestion. "I am cold," says the "I" of metabolism. "No one will stop me," exclaims the passionate "I" when in defense of the other loose cathexes.

Conclusion, the "I" is a legion of loose cathexes. These loose cathexes have already been studied by Franz Hartmann. They live in the lower animal depths of the human being; they eat, sleep, reproduce, and live at the expense of our vital principles or free cathexis (muscular and nervous kinetic energy). Each of the "I's" (which in their conjunction constitute the loose cathexis or the "I") projects itself in the different levels of the mind and travels, longing for the satisfaction of its desires. The "I", the ego, the loose cathexis, can never perfect itself.

The human being is the city of nine gates... Within this city live many citizens who do not even know each other. Each of these citizens, each of those small "I's," has its own projects and its own mind; those are the merchants that Jesus had to cast out of the temple with the whip of willpower. Those merchants must be killed.

Now we will understand the reason for so many internal contradictions in the individual. As long as the loose cathexis exists, there can be no peace. The "I's" are the *causa causorum* of all our internal contradictions. The "I" that swears fidelity to Gnosis is replaced by another that hates it! Conclusion, the present human being is an irresponsible entity who does not have a Permanent Center of Gravity. The present human being is a being that is not yet completed!

The present manlike being is not yet human; he is merely an intellectual animal. It is a very grave error to call the legion of the "I" the "soul." In fact, what the manlike being has is the psychic material, the material for the soul within his Essence, but indeed, he does not have a Soul yet.

The Gospels state, *"Of what use is it to win the world if you are going to lose your soul?"* Jesus told Nicodemus that it is necessary to be born from water and the spirit in order to enjoy the attributes that correspond to a true soul. It is impossible to fabricate a soul if we do not undergo Mystical Death.

It is only through the death of the "I" that we can establish a Permanent Center of Consciousness within our own interior Essence; such center is called a Soul. Only a human being with a Soul can have true continuity of purpose. It is only

THE MYSTICAL DEATH OF JOHN THE BAPTIST. ENGRAVING BY ALBRECHT DÜRER.

within a human being who has a Soul that internal contradictions do not exist. True inner peace exists within him.

The "I" foolishly spends the psychic material, the cathexis, in explosions of anger, covetousness, lust, envy, pride, laziness, gluttony, etc. It is logical that as long as the psychic material, the cathexis, does not accumulate, the Soul cannot be fabricated. In order to fabricate something, one needs the raw matter; without the raw matter, nothing can be fabricated, because from nothing, nothing can be obtained.

When the "I" begins to die, the raw matter begins to accumulate. When the raw matter begins to accumulate, the establishment of a Center of Permanent Consciousness is initiated. When the "I" has absolutely died, the Center of Permanent Consciousness has been totally established.

The capital of psychic material accumulates when the ego dies since the squanderer of energy is eliminated. In this manner, the Permanent Center of Consciousness is established. Such a marvelous center is the Soul.

Only the one who has established within himself the Permanent Center of Consciousness can be faithful to Gnosis;

only he can have continuity of purpose. Those who do not possess such a center can be in Gnosis today and against it tomorrow; today with one school, tomorrow with another. This type of person does not have a real existence.

Mystical death is an arduous and difficult area of the revolution of the dialectic.

The loose cathexis is dissolved on the basis of rigorous comprehension. Interaction with our fellowmen, dealing with people, is the mirror in which we can see ourselves at full length. In dealing with people our hidden defects leap forth, they flourish, and if we are vigilant, we can then see them.

Every defect must first be intellectually analyzed and then studied with meditation.

Many individuals attained perfect chastity in the physical world, but ended up being great fornicators and frightening sinners when they were subjected to the test in the superior worlds. They had put an end to their defects in the physical world, but in other levels of the mind, they continued with their loose cathexis.

When a defect is totally comprehended in all the levels of the mind, its corresponding loose cathexis disintegrates, in other words, a small "I" dies.

It is urgent to die from moment to moment. The Soul is born with the death of the "I." We need the death of the "I" in a total manner in order for the plenitude of the bound cathexis, the Being, to express himself.

Dissolving the Loose Cathexis

It is only by minutely studying the loose cathexis, or the "I," that we can totally dissolve it.

We must minutely observe the thought processes, the different functionalisms of desire, the habits that form our personality, the sophisms of distraction, the fallacy of the ego, and our sexual impulses. We have to study how they react before the impacts of the exterior world and see how they associate with each other.

By comprehending all the processes of the loose cathexis, of the pluralized "I," the latter is dissolved. Only then is the Divinity manifested through and within us.

Negligence

Negligence and carelessness lead every human being to failure.

To be negligent is, as we would say, *nec legere*, "to not elect," to surrender to the arms of failure.

Negligence is of the ego, and its opposite is intuition, which is of the Being. The ego can neither elect nor distinguish, but the Being can.

It is only by means of the living incarnation of the revolution of the dialectic that we will learn to "elect" in order not to have any more failures in life.

Transactions

Ninety-seven percent of human thoughts are negative and harmful.

What we are in this world is the result of our own mental processes.

If the human being wishes to identify himself, to value himself, and to imagine himself correctly, then he must explore his own mind.

The difficulty of profound introspective analysis lies in "counter-transference." This difficulty is eliminated through structural and transactional analysis.

It is important to segregate and to dissolve certain undesirable psychic aggregates that are fixed in our mind in a traumatic manner.

Transactional and structural analyses are combined in the matter of the exploration of the ego.

Any psychic aggregate must be previously segregated before its final dissolution.

The Particular Characteristic Psychological Feature

All human beings are one hundred percent mechanical, unconscious beings. Because they are profoundly hypnotized, they work with their consciousness asleep without ever knowing where they come from or where they are going.

The hypnosis (which is collective and flows in all of nature) is derived from the abominable Kundabuffer organ. The present human race is hypnotized and unconscious; it is submerged in the most profound sleep.

Awakening is only possible by destroying the "I," the ego. We have to recognize with complete clarity that each person has his own Particular Characteristic Psychological Feature (PCPF), which we have spoken about many times before.

Certainly, each person has his own particular characteristic psychological feature, this is a fact. Some will have lust as their characteristic feature; others will have hatred; for others it will be covetousness, etc. The feature is the sum of several particular characteristic psychological elements.

For each PCPF, a definitive event, a precise circumstance, always occurs. What if a man is lustful? There will always be circumstances of lust in his life accompanied by specific problems. These circumstances are always repeated.

We need to know our PCPF if we want to move on to a superior level of the Being and eliminate from within ourselves the undesirable elements that constitute our psychological feature.

It is obvious that there exists a concrete fact in life; it is the discontinuity of nature.

All phenomena are discontinuous; this signifies that we will never arrive at perfection through evolution. We need to become true Solar Men in the most complete sense of the word.

Have we perceived our own level of Being, the level of the Being in which we are? Are we conscious that we are hypnotized and asleep? Different levels of the Being exist. For instance, the level of the worthy and modest woman is one level; the level of the unworthy and immodest woman is another.

The intellectual animal becomes identified not only with external things, but he also goes around identified with himself, with his lustful thoughts, with his drunken sprees, with his anger, with his covetousness, with his self-importance, with his vanity, with mystical pride, with self-merit, etc.

Have we perhaps reflected upon the fact that we have not only become identified with the external world but also with our internal vanity and pride? For example: did we triumph today? Did we triumph over the day or did the day triumph over us? Are we sure that we did not become identified with a morbid, covetous, proud thought, with an insult or a preoccupation or a debt, etc.? Are we sure that we triumphed over the day or did the day triumph over us?

What did we do today? Have we perceived the level of the Being in which we are? Did we move on to a superior level of the Being or did we remain where we were?

Can we perhaps believe that it is possible to move on to a superior level of the Being if we do not eliminate specific psychological defects? Are we perhaps content with the level of the Being in which we presently find ourselves? If we are going to remain in one level of the Being for our entire life, then what are we doing?

It is obvious that in each level of the Being there exists specific bitterness and specific sufferings. Everyone complains about how he suffers, about how he has problems, about the state he is in and about his struggles. Therefore, I ask one thing: does the intellectual animal concern himself with moving on to a superior level of Being?

Obviously, as long as we are in the level of Being in which we are, all the adverse circumstances that we already know and all the bitterness in which we are will have to be repeated again. Over and over again, identical difficulties will surge.

Do we want to change? Do we want to no longer have the problems that afflict us, the economical, political, social, spiritual, familial, lustful problems, etc.? Do we want to avoid difficulties? Then, we have no other solution but to move on to a superior level of Being.

Each time that we take a step towards a superior level of the Being, we become independent of the executing forces of the loose cathexis.

Therefore, if we do not know our PCPF we are doing very badly. We need to know it if we want to move on to a superior level of Being. We need to know it if we want to eliminate from ourselves the undesirable elements that constitute our PCPF, otherwise how will we move on to a superior level of the Being?

The intellectual animal wants to stop suffering but he does nothing to change; he does not struggle to move on to a superior level of Being. Therefore, how can he change?

All phenomena are discontinuous; therefore any change through the dogma of evolution serves no purpose except to stagnate us. I know many pseudo-esotericists who are sincere people and of good heart. However, they are bottled up in the dogma of evolution. They wait for time to perfect them and millions of years elapse and they never perfect themselves. Why? Because such people do nothing in order to change the level of their Being; they always remain on the same rung. Therefore, we need to go beyond evolution and enter onto the revolutionary path, the path of the revolution of the consciousness or of the dialectic.

Evolution and devolution are the two laws that are simultaneously processed in all of creation; these laws constitute the mechanical axis of nature. Nevertheless, these laws will never lead us towards liberation.

The laws of evolution and devolution are in every way related to matter and have nothing to do with the inner Self-realization of the Being. We do not deny these laws, they exist, but they are worthless for psychological revolution. We need to be revolutionary and enter the path of the revolution of the consciousness.

How could we move in to a level of the Being if we are not revolutionary? Let us observe the different rungs of a ladder. The rungs are discontinuous, as are the different levels of the Being.

A number of activities belong to each level of the Being. When one moves to a higher level of the Being, one has to take a leap and abandon all the activities that one had in the inferior level of the Being.

Into my memory come all those times of my life, twenty, thirty, forty years ago, that were transcended. Why? It is because I found superior levels of the Being.

The activities of those times were what constituted for me the highest priority. However, my activities of that era were suspended, cut off, because in the superior rungs of the Being there are other activities that are completely different.

If one moves into a superior level of the Being, then many things that are presently important to oneself have to be left behind, because those things belong to the level in which we were.

Therefore, the psychological transaction into another level of the Being includes a leap. That is a rebellious leap; it is never of an evolving type, it is always a revolutionary dialectic leap.

There exist presumptuous people who feel that they are like gods; these types of individuals are mythomaniacs of the worst kind, of the worst taste. The one who feels he is a sage because he has some pseudo-esoteric teachings in his mind and thinks that he is already a great Initiate has fallen into mythomania; he is full of himself.

Each one of us is nothing but a vile slug in the mud of the earth. When I speak in this manner, I begin with myself. To be full of oneself, to have false images of oneself, fantasies of oneself, is to be in the inferior levels of the Being.

One is identified with oneself when one thinks that one is going to have a lot of money, the beautiful, latest model car, or to think that one's fiancée loves him, that one is a great person, or that one is a sage. There are many forms of becoming identified with oneself. One has to begin by not becoming identified with oneself, and afterwards, not becoming identified with external things.

For example, when one does not become identified with an offender, one forgives him and loves him; the offender cannot hurt us. Thus, if someone hurts one's self esteem, yet one does not become identified with one's self-esteem, it is therefore clear that one cannot feel any pain because one was not hurt.

If one does not become identified with vanity, one does not care about walking on the street even with mended trousers. Why? It is because one is not identified with vanity.

We cannot forgive our fellowmen if we first become identified with ourselves and then with the vanities of the exterior world. Let us remember the Lord's Prayer, *"Forgive us our trespasses as we forgive those who trespass against us..."* Yet, I say something more has to be done, because it is not enough to simply forgive. We have to also cancel the debts. Someone could forgive an enemy but would never ever cancel the debt. Therefore, we have to be sincere, we need to cancel...

The Lord's Gospel also states, *"Blessed are the meek for they will inherit the earth..."* This is a phrase that no one understands. Blessed are, we would say, the non-resentful. If one is resentful how could one be meek? The resentful person delights in keeping count. He says, "And I who did him so many favors... who protected him, who did so many deeds of charity for him... and look how this friend has paid me back, when I have helped him so much and now he is incapable of helping me!" This is the "accounting" of the resentful.

How could one be meek if one is full of resentments? The one who is full of resentments lives keeping count at all times, therefore he is not meek. How could he be blessed?

What is understood by blessed? What is understood by happiness? Are we sure that we are happy? Who is happy? I have known people who say, "I am happy! I am content with my life! I am joyful!" But I have heard these same people say, "Such a fellow bothers me! I dislike that person! I do not know why I cannot get what I have always desired!" Therefore, they are not happy; what really happens is that they are hypocrites, that is all.

To be happy is very difficult; for that, one first of all needs to be meek.

The word *beatitude* means inner happiness, not in a thousand years, but now, right here, in the instant we are living.

If we truly become meek through non-identification, we will then get to be happy. But it is necessary not only to not become identified with our thoughts of lust, hatred, vengeance, rancor, resentment, but also to eliminate from ourselves the Red Demons of Seth, those psychic aggregates that personify our defects of a psychological type.

We have to comprehend, for example, the process of resentment; we have to dissect resentment. When one arrives at the conclusion that resentment is due to possessing self-esteem in our interior, we then struggle to eliminate the "I" of self-esteem. But we have to comprehend it in order to be able to eliminate it; we could not eliminate it if we have not previously comprehended it.

In order to be able to eliminate, one needs Devi Kundalini Shakti; it is only she who can disintegrate any psychological defect, including the "I" of self-esteem.

Are we sure that we are not resentful towards someone? Which of us is sure of not being resentful and of not keeping count? Who?

If we want to become independent from lunar mechanicity, we have to eliminate from ourselves the "I" of resentment

The Divine Mother (depicted here in Hinduism as Kali) utilizes transmuted sexual fire to destroy the ego and recover the energy of the loose cathexis (symbolized by the blood). Around her neck are the heads of the conquered egos.

and of self-esteem. When one understands this, one advances on the path that leads to final Liberation.

It is only by means of the fire of Aries, the Lamb of the incarnated Ram, of the Intimate Christ, that we can truly burn those elements that we carry within our interior. Thus, we will continue awakening in the same measure that the consciousness releases itself from being bottled up.

Consciousness cannot awaken as long as it continues being bottled up within the psychic aggregates, which in their conjunction constitute the myself, the "I," the loose cathexis. We need to undergo a mystical death here and now. We need to die from moment to moment; only with death can the new arrive. If the seed does not die, the plant cannot be born. We need to learn to live, to liberate ourselves from the lunar heredity that we have.

Methodology of the Work

Before knowing and eliminating the PCPF, we should work intensely in a general manner in relation to all the defects since the PCPF has very profound roots that come from past existences. In order to know it, it is necessary to have worked in an untiring manner with a methodology of work for at least five years.

We must have order in the work and precision in the elimination of our defects. For example, on any given day the defects of lust might have manifested themselves through us in the morning, the defects of pride in the afternoon and the defects of anger at night. Indubitably, we are seeing a succession of facts and manifestations. Therefore, we ask ourselves: on which defect should we work on and how should we work on this defect that manifested itself through us during the day?

In fact, this is indeed simple. At nightfall or at the hour of meditation, we move on to practice the retrospective exercise (with the body relaxed) on the facts and manifestations of the ego during that day. Once reconstructed, in order and numbered, we proceed with the work of comprehension.

First we will work on an egotistical event to which we could dedicate some twenty minutes, then another psychological event to which we could dedicate ten minutes, and fifteen minutes to yet another manifestation. The amount of time needed depends on the gravity and intensity of the egotistical events.

Once the facts and manifestations of the loose cathexis, of the myself, have been put in order, we can work on them at night or during the hour of meditation, in a tranquil manner and with methodical order.

Into each work performed on this or that defect, on this or that event, or on this or that manifestation enter the following factors: discovery, judgment, and execution.

The three aforementioned factors are applied to each psychological defect in the following manner:

> **Discovery:** when the ego has been seen in action, in manifestation.
>
> **Judgment or comprehension:** when all of the ego's roots are known.
>
> **Execution:** with the help of the Divine Mother Kundalini, through the wise practice of Sexual Super-dynamics, the ego is eliminated.

Sophisms of Distraction

Sophisms are the false reasonings that induce us to err and that are gestated by the ego in the forty-nine levels of the subconsciousness.

The subconsciousness is the sepulcher of the past upon which burns the fatuous fire of thought and in which the sophisms of distraction are gestated; the latter lead the intellectual animal to fascination, and thereby, to the sleep of the consciousness.

What is kept within the sepulcher is decay and the bones of the dead, but the sepulchral stone is very beautiful and on it fatally burns the flame of the intellect.

If we want to dissolve the "I," we have to uncover the subconsciousness' sepulcher and exhume all the bones and decay of the past. The sepulcher is very beautiful on the outside, but within, it is filthy and abominable; we need to become gravediggers.

To insult another person, to hurt his intimate feelings, to humiliate him, is something that is very easy when it is done supposedly to correct him for his own good. This is how irate people think, those who while believing that they do not hate, hate without knowing that they hate.

Many are the people who struggle in life to be rich. They work, save, and strive for excellence in everything, but the secret trigger of all their activities is secret envy, which is ignored, which does not come to the surface, which remains hidden within the sepulcher of their subconsciousness.

In life, it is difficult to find someone who does not envy the beautiful house, the brand new car, the intelligence of the leader, the beautiful suit, the good social position, the magnificent fortune, etc.

Almost always, the best efforts of citizens have envy as their secret trigger.

Many are the people who enjoy a good appetite and despise gluttony, but they always eat more than normal.

Many are the people who watch their spouse in an exaggerated manner, but they despise jealousy.

Many are the students of certain pseudo-esoteric and pseudo-occultist schools who despise the things of this world; they do not work at all because they believe everything is vanity, yet they are zealous of their virtues and never accept anyone classifying them as lazy people.

Many are those who hate flattery and praise, but they have no inconvenience in humiliating with their modesty the poor poet who composed a verse for them with the sole purpose of obtaining a coin to buy bread.

Many are the judges who know how to fulfill their duty, but also, many are the judges who with their virtue of duty have assassinated others. Numerous were the heads that fell by the guillotine of the French Revolution.

All executioners fulfill their duty and millions are their innocent victims. No executioner feels himself to be guilty; they are all just "fulfilling their duty..."

Prisons are full of innocent people, but the judges do not feel guilty because they are "fulfilling their duty."

Filled with anger, the father or mother whip and beat their small children, but they do not feel remorse because supposedly they are fulfilling their duty and they would accept everything except being classified as being cruel.

It is only with a still and silent mind, submerged in profound meditation, that we will be able to extract from within the sepulcher of the subconsciousness all the secret rottenness that we carry within. It is nothing pleasant to see the dark sepulcher with all the bones and rottenness of the past.

Each hidden defect smells awful inside its grave. However, when seeing it, it is easy to burn it and reduce it to ashes.

The fire of comprehension reduces to dust the decay of the past. Many students of psychology, when they analyze their subconsciousness, commit the mistake of dividing themselves between analyzer and analyzed, intellect and subconsciousness, subject and object, perceiver and perceived. [Editor: see *Separation* in the Glossary.]

Those types of divisions are the sophisms of distraction that the ego presents to us. These types of divisions create antagonisms and struggles between the intellect and the subconsciousness, and where there are struggles and battles there cannot be stillness and silence of the mind.

It is only in mental stillness and silence that we can extract from within the dark grave of the subconsciousness all the rottenness of the past.

Let us not say "my I has envy, hatred, jealousy, anger, lust," etc., it is best to not divide ourselves; it is better to say: "I have envy, hatred, jealousy, anger, lust," etc.

When we study the sacred books of India, we become enthusiastic thinking about the supreme Brahma and in the union of Atman with Brahma. Nevertheless, as long as a psychological "I" with its sophisms of distraction exists, indeed we will be unable to achieve the bliss of uniting ourselves with the Universal Spirit of Life. Once the "I" is dead, the Universal Spirit of Life is in us like the flame of a lamp.

The Fallacy of the Ego

The fallacy of the ego is the habit of deceiving without any limitations; this fallacy is processed through the series of the "I."

Any person can commit the error of shooting himself in the head (as is done by any cowardly and imbecilic suicidal person) but the famous "I" of psychology will never be able to commit suicide.

People of all pseudo-esoteric schools have magnificent ideals and even sublime intentions. However, all of these ideals and sublime intentions sustain their existence in the field of subjective and miserable thinking, because all of that belongs to the "I."

The "I" is always perverse; sometimes it adorns itself with beautiful virtues and even wears the robe of sanctity.

When the "I" wants to cease to exist, it does not do it in a disinterested and pure manner; it wants to continue in a different manner; it aspires for reward and happiness.

During these mechanized times of life, there is production of series: series of cars, series of airplanes, series of machines of this or that brand, etc.; everything has become a series and even the "I" itself is a series.

Every one who exalts himself will be humbled, but he
who humbles himself with be exalted.

THE PARABLE OF THE PUBLICAN AND THE PHARISEE,
LUKE 18:10-14. ENGRAVING BY J. VON CAROLFELD.

We must know the series of the "I." The "I" processes itself in series and more series of thoughts, sentiments, desires, hatreds, habits, etc.

Let those who divide the "I" continue dividing their ego between "superior and inferior"; let them go on with their theories and their boasted superior and ultra-divine "I" controlling their miserable inferior "I."

We know very well that such a division between the superior "I" and the inferior "I" is one hundred percent false. Superior and inferior are two sections of the same thing. Superior "I" and inferior "I" are the two sections of Satan, the "I."

Can perhaps a part of the "I" reduce another part of the "I" to dust? Can perhaps one part of the myself decree the law of exile to another part of the myself?

The most we can do is to astutely conceal what is convenient for us; to hide our perversities and smile like saints.

This is what the fallacy of the ego is. This is the habit of deceiving. One part of the myself can hide another part of the myself. Is this something unusual? Does not the cat hide his claws? This is what the fallacy of the ego is. We all carry the Pharisee within us; we are very beautiful from the outside, but we are very rotten on the inside.

We have known Pharisees who are horrifying. We knew one who wore the immaculate robe of the Master, his hair was long and a razor never shaved his venerable beard. This man frightened the entire world with his sanctity; he was one hundred percent vegetarian; he drank nothing that could have alcohol. People knelt before him.

We do not mention the name of this "hypocritical saint." We only limit ourselves to say that he had abandoned his wife and children supposedly to follow the path of sanctity.

He preached beautiful things and spoke horrors against adultery and fornication, yet in secrecy, he had many concubines. To his female devotees he proposed anti-natural intimate relations through non-appropriate vessels. Yes, he was a saint, a "hypocritical saint!"

This is how Pharisees are...

Woe unto you scribes and Pharisees, hypocrites! For ye make clean the outside of the cup and of the platter, but within ye are full of extortion and excess.

You do not eat meat, you do not drink alcohol, you do not smoke... Truly you appear just before men, but you are filled with hypocrisy and evil within.

With his fallacy of the ego, the Pharisee conceals the crimes from the eyes of others, and also conceals them from himself.

We know Pharisees who carry out tremendous fasts and frightening acts of penance; they are convinced of being just and wise, but their victims suffer the unutterable. Almost always, it is their wives and their children who are innocent victims of their evil deeds. Nevertheless, they continue with their sacred exercises convinced of being just and holy.

The so-called superior "I" says: "I will overcome anger, covetousness, lust," etc.., but the so-called inferior "I" then laughs with the thunderous laughter of Aristophanes and the demons of passions; terrified, they flee to hide themselves within the caverns of the different areas of the mind. This is how the fallacy of the ego functions.

Every intellectual effort to dissolve the "I" is useless because any movement of the mind belongs to the "I." Any part of the myself can have good intentions, so what? The path that leads to the abyss is paved with good intentions.

That game or fallacy in which one part of the myself wants to control another part of the myself (that has no desire of being controlled) is interesting.

Touching are the acts of penance of those saints who cause their wife and children to suffer. All those humilities of "self-proclaimed saints" are funny. Admirable is the erudition of those know-it-alls, but so what? The "I" cannot destroy the "I" and it continues perpetuating itself through millions of years in our descendants.

We must break the spell of all those useless efforts and fallacies. When the "I" wants to destroy the "I," it is a useless effort.

It is only by truly comprehending in depth what the useless battles of the mind are; it is only by comprehending the internal and external actions and reactions, the secret answers, the hidden motives, the concealed impulses, etc., that we can then attain the imposing stillness and silence of the mind.

Upon the pure waters of the ocean of the Universal Mind, we can contemplate in a state of ecstasy all the devilries of the pluralized "I."

When the "I" can no longer hide, it is condemned to death. The "I" likes to hide, but when it can no longer hide, this wretched one is lost.

It is only in the serenity of the mind that we see the "I" just as it is and not as it apparently is. To see the "I" and comprehend it becomes an integral whole. The "I" has failed after we have comprehended it because it inevitably becomes dust.

The stillness of the ocean of the mind is not a result, it is a natural state. The swollen waves of thoughts are only an accident produced by a monster, which is the "I."

The fatuous mind, the stubborn mind, the mind that says, "With time I will achieve serenity, one day I will get there," is condemned to failure because the serenity of the mind does not belong to time. Everything that belongs to time is of the "I." The "I" itself is of time.

Those who want to assemble the serenity of the mind, to assemble it like someone who assembles a machine by intelligently joining all of its parts, are in fact failures, because the serenity of the mind is not constituted by several parts that can be assembled, organized or disorganized, joined or separated.

Exertion

In order to experience the truth, one does not need to exert oneself whatsoever. People are accustomed to exerting themselves in everything they do and erroneously suppose that it is impossible to experience the truth without any exertion.

We may need to exert ourselves in order to earn our daily bread, to play a game of football, or to carry a very heavy load. But it is absurd to believe that exertion is necessary in order to experience that which is the truth.

Comprehension replaces **exertion** when one tries to comprehend the truth intimately hidden in the secret depths of each problem.

We do not need any exertion to comprehend each and every defect that we carry hidden within the different levels of the mind.

We do not need exertion in order to comprehend that envy is one of the most powerful triggers of social machinery. Why do so many people want to progress? Why do so many people want to have beautiful residences and very elegant cars? The entire world envies what belongs to others. Envy is regret for others' well-being.

Elegant women are envied by other less elegant women and this serves to intensify their struggle and pain. Those who do not have, want to have, and will choose to not eat in order to buy all types of clothes and adornments. They do this with the sole objective of not being less than anyone else.

Every paladin of a great cause is mortally hated by the envious. The envy of the impotent, of the vanquished, of the mean person, is disguised with the judge's toga, or with the robe of sanctity and of mastery, or with the sophism of applause, or with the beauty of humility.

If we integrally comprehend that we are envious, it is logical that envy will then end and in its place will appear the star that rejoices and shines for others' well-being.

There are people who want to cease being covetous but who covet not being covetous; there you have a form of covetousness.

There are men who exert themselves in order to attain the virtue of chastity, but when they see a beautiful woman on the street, they pay her beautiful compliments; and if the woman is a friend, they can do nothing less than ply her with attention, say beautiful words to her, admire her, praise her beautiful qualities, etc. The secret intentions behind all of that coquetry are found in the secret trigger of the subconsciousness: tenebrous and submerged lust.

When we comprehend without any exertion whatsoever all the tricks of lust, the latter is annihilated and in its place is born the immaculate flower of chastity.

It is not with any exertion that we can acquire those virtues. The "I" is fortified when it exerts itself to acquire virtues. The "I" loves decorations, medals, titles, honors, virtues, beautiful qualities, etc.

Greek traditions narrate that Aristippus, the philosopher, wanting to demonstrate his wisdom and modesty, put on an old robe full of patches and holes, clutched the staff of philosophy and walked down the streets of Athens. When Socrates saw him arrive at his house, he exclaimed, "Oh, Aristippus, one can see your vanity through the holes of your vesture."

Thus, this is how, when wearing the robe of Aristippus, the pedantic, the vain and proud ones believe themselves to be very humble. Humility is a very exotic flower; whosoever boasts of humility is full of pride.

In practical life, each time a new problem torments us, we make many useless exertions. We appeal to exertions to solve it; we struggle and suffer, but then, the only thing that we obtain is to commit inanities and to complicate our existence even more.

The disillusioned, the disenchanted ones, those who no longer even want to think, those who were not able to solve a vital problem, find the solution to it when their mind is serene and tranquil, when they have had no hope whatsoever.

No truth can be comprehended by means of exertion. The truth comes like a thief in the night, when one least expects it.

Extrasensory perceptions during meditation, illumination, the solution to a problem, are only possible when no kind of conscious or subconscious exertion exists, when the mind does not exert itself to be more than it is.

Pride also disguises itself as being sublime; the mind exerts itself to be something more than it is. The mind, serene like a lake, can experience the truth; but when the mind wants to be something more, it is in tension, it is in struggle and then the experience of the truth becomes impossible.

We should not mistake the truth with opinions. Many think that the truth is this or that, or that the truth is within this or that book, or within this or that belief or idea, etc.

Whosoever wants to experience the truth should not mistake beliefs, ideas, opinions, and theories with that which is the truth.

We must experience the truth in a direct, practical, and real manner; this is only possible in the stillness and silence of the mind, and this is achieved by means of meditation.

To experience the truth is fundamental. It is not by means of exertion that we can experience the truth. The truth is not the result; the truth is not the product of exertion. The truth comes to us by means of profound comprehension.

We need to exert ourselves in order to work in the Great Work and to transmute our creative energies. We need to exert ourselves to live, to struggle and to tread the path of integral revolution, but we do not need to exert ourselves in order to comprehend the truth.

Psychological Slavery

The reason why we have written this book entitled *The Revolution of the Dialectic* is because there is not even the least bit of doubt that we are on the verge of a third world conflagration.

Times have changed and we are initiating a new era within the august thundering of thought. A new revolutionary ethic based on a revolutionary psychology is now needed.

Without an in-depth ethic, the best social and economic formulae remain reduced to dust. It is impossible for the individual to transform himself if he does not concern himself with the dissolution of the "I."

Psychological slavery destroys interaction. Psychological dependence on someone is slavery. If our manner of thinking, feeling, and acting depends on the manner of thinking, feeling, and acting of those people who interact with us, then we are enslaved.

We constantly receive letters from many people who are desirous of eliminating the "I," but they complain about their wives, children, brothers, families, husbands, bosses, etc. Those people demand certain conditions in order to dissolve the "I." They want luxuries in order to annihilate the ego; they demand magnificent conduct from those with whom they interact.

The funniest thing of all in this matter is that those poor people seek different subterfuges; they want to flee, abandon their home, their job, etc., supposedly to self-realize themselves in depth.

Wretched people... Naturally, their adored torments exert command over them. These people have not yet learned to be free; their conduct depends on the conduct of others.

If we want to follow the path of chastity and aspire that our spouse first be chaste, then we are failures already. We want to cease being drunkards but when others offer us a drink we accept it because we are embarrassed to be considered "such a square," or because our friends could become angry with us; we will never cease to be drunkards in this way.

If we want to cease being angry, irascible, irate, furious, but as a prior condition we demand that those who interact with us be sweet and serene so that they won't do anything to bother us, then indeed we are failures because others are not saints. Thus, at any moment, they will put an end to our good intentions.

If we want to dissolve the "I," we need to be free. The one who depends on the behavior of others will not be able to dissolve the "I." Our conduct must be our own and must not depend on anyone. Our thoughts, feelings, and actions must flow independently from the inside to the outside.

The worst difficulties offer us the best opportunities. In the past there existed many sages surrounded by all types of luxuries who were without any type of difficulties. Wanting to annihilate the "I," those sages had to create difficult situations for themselves.

In difficult situations we have formidable opportunities to study our internal and external impulses: our thoughts, sentiments, actions, our reactions, volitions, etc.

Interaction is a full-length mirror in which we can see ourselves as we are and not as we apparently seem to be. Interaction is a marvel. If we are properly attentive at each moment we can discover our most secret defects; they flourish and leap out when we least expect it.

We have known many people who say, "I no longer have anger," however, at the least provocation they thunder and flash like lightning. Others say, "I no longer have jealousy," however, only one smile from their spouse to any good neighbor is enough for their faces to become green with jealousy.

People protest because of the difficulties that interaction offers them. They do not want to realize that those difficulties are precisely providing them with the necessary opportunities for the dissolution of their "I." Interaction is a formidable school; the book of that school is made up of many chapters; the book of that school is the "I."

We need to be really free if we want to truly dissolve the "I." The one who depends on the conduct of others is not free. Only the one who becomes truly free knows what love is. The slave does not know what true love is. If we are slaves of the thinking, feeling, and action of others, we will never know what love is.

Love is born in us when we put an end to psychological slavery. We need to very profoundly comprehend, in all the levels of the mind, the entire complicated mechanism of psychological slavery.

There are many forms of psychological slavery. If we really want to dissolve the "I," then it is necessary to study all those forms of psychological slavery.

Psychological slavery exists not only internally but also externally. Intimate, secret, occult slavery exists that we do not even remotely suspect.

The slave believes that he loves, yet in reality he only fears, because the slave does not know what true love is.

The woman who fears her husband believes that she adores him, when truly she only fears him. The husband who fears his wife believes that he loves her when in reality what is happening is that he fears her. He may fear that she may leave with someone else, or that her character may become sour, or that sexually she may deny him, etc.

The employee who fears his boss believes that he loves him, that he respects him, that he cares for his interests, etc.

No psychological slave knows what love is. Psychological slavery is incompatible with love.

There are two types of conduct: the first one comes from the outside and goes towards the inside; the second one goes from the inside and goes towards the outside. The first is the result of psychological slavery and is produced by reaction; for example, we are hit and we hit back; we are insulted and we reply with insults. The best type of conduct is the second, that of the one who is no longer a slave; that of the one who no longer has anything to do with the thinking, feeling, and doings of others. That type of conduct is independent; it is upright and just conduct. If we are hit, we answer with blessings; if we are insulted, we keep silent. If they want to get us drunk, we do not drink even though our friends become angry, etc.

Now our readers will comprehend why psychological freedom brings us that which is called love.

The Kalkian Personality

Each day we must become more and more conscious of the work that we are doing. Therefore, it is fundamental to know the differences that exist between the Gnostic Movement and all the other pseudo-esoteric and pseudo-occultist organizations that we find in the world today. If we want to comprehend the work that we must do, we have to know how to situate ourselves, how to center ourselves, above all else.

If we take a general look at the different pseudo-esoteric and pseudo-occultist schools that presently exist in the world, we can easily discover their origin.

On one occasion in Rome, Italy, there occurred the case of a nun who constantly fell into a hypnotic trance. She confessed and clarified the *causa causorum* of those fatal trances to a priest. First of all, the priest managed to figure out that she had had a lover and that although she was cloistered, she kept a photograph of her lover with her. The priest made her bring the photograph to him. He suddenly realized that just by merely looking at that picture, the nun would fall into a trance. The priest asked for assistance from a psychologist in order for him to perform some psychic experiments on the nun. Afterwards, they realized that it was not the photograph of the man that put the nun into a trance, but rather some very shiny stones that were around the picture frame.

The investigations continued and very soon it was possible to conclude, as a consequence or corollary, that all types of brilliant objects predispose people to fall into hypnotic states. As a result, an entire school was formed on that finding. They were able to verify that by means of hypnotic states, it would be possible to modify, in some way, the psychological states of patients. It was thereby resolved that hypnosis should be use to cure patients or sick people.

This is how the famous medical hypnotists were born. It was then that many followers of hypnology, catalepsy, mediumism, etc. made their appearance in the world. It is not irrelevant to remember Richard Charcott, Luis Uribe, Cesar Lombroso, Camile Flammarion, etc. with certain emphasis.

In that school of hypnotists, an Englishman (whose name I do not recall in this precise moment) and the famous Charcott are the ones who especially stood out. The Englishman had all the properties of a Hanasmuss, and Charcott was no doubt "a momma's boy." He was the "baby" of the family, the spoiled child, and everything that he did was a marvel. He did, however, have some noteworthy experiments.

If I generally mention any of these passages and experiments of magnetism, hypnology, catalepsy, Spiritism (and fifty thousand other things of that sort) it is to make you see where the different pseudo-esotericism and pseudo-occultism schools come from in this dark age of Kali Yuga.

It was during the time when Oriental Theosophy began to emerge that a famous phantom named Katie King materialized for three consecutive years in front of the eyes of many scientists of the world through the young ladies Fox of Mirville (mediums). It was in those days when all of Europe became agitated with psychic phenomena, especially that of Eusapia Paladino of Naples. Anyone who has visited any of those types of organizations knows that there always exists a mixture of Spiritism with Hindu-type theories. Theosophy has never been free of the spiritualistic phenomenon.

When we know the origin of the different organizations that presently exist, it cannot surprise us in any way that Theosophy is mixed with some form of medium-channeling.

That fact that Theosophists become frightened when facing Tantra is normal because it is not a school of an esoteric type, but rather a school of a pseudo-occultist type and nothing more.

Unquestionably, many branches or organizations (let's call them pseudo-rosicrucianism, pseudo-yogism, etc.) had to branch off, as is natural, from that school of hypnotists. These branches are so innumerable that we would need to consult an encyclopedia to find out all of their names.

But let us get to the bottom of this subject matter. What is the foundation of such schools? It is *the dogma of evolution*. From where did such boasted dogma come from? It comes from Mr. Darwin, of course.

It seems incredible that Mr. Darwin has put into his pocket many eminent figures, many esotericists, pseudo-esotericist investigators, and many sincere aspirants. But we cannot deny how it happened.

The concept of reincarnation that was created by those pseudo-esoteric organizations in the western world is false. Lord Krishna never said that all human beings reincarnate. He said that only the Buddhas, the Gods, the solar Heroes, have the right to reincarnate. It is clear that the rest of us are subjected to the Law of the Eternal Return of all things.

In the East it was also never said that all humanoid beings possess the superior existential bodies of the Being. Nevertheless, it was easy for the pseudo-esoteric and pseudo-occultist schools to make humanity believe that the entire world already possesses such superior vehicles. In this manner, they speak about the subject of "the septenary of man" with such certainty and confidence that it seems as if all humanoids truly possess that entire set of vehicles.

Therefore, the Kalkian personality (the personality that is characteristic of this Kali Yuga) is the outcome of all this sort of morbid knowledge that was disseminated throughout the western world in all of these subjective, incoherent, vague, and indefinite schools.

Kalkian personalities are disrespectful, irreverent. This type of personality from these pseudo-esoteric and pseudo-occultist schools has lost not only the sense of authentic devotion and of true religiosity but also that of veneration for the ancient Patriarchs. In this manner, humanity (having been able to be directed by truly wise religions) has degenerated in its ridiculous pedantry, thus forming the Kalkian personality.

It is convenient to know how to confront a Kalkian personality with an authentic esoteric personality. What is the difference? The Kalkian personality is full of pedantries; it is bottled up in the dogma of evolution, misinformed about the internal constitution of the human being. The Kalkian personality ignores the Tantric mysteries. The Kalkian personality fears the development of the igneous serpent in the spinal column, besides the fact of being stuffed with theories, which produces a feeling of self-sufficiency.

Unquestionably, the Kalkian personalities are victims of self-deceit. They believe that they have achieved everything when indeed they have achieved nothing, and what is worse is that they have lost their sense of veneration. They have forgotten the true and authentic religiosity. They have also lost their humility before the Creator Logos. This is what the Kalkian personalities are.

We cannot walk on the path of the Kalkian personality. We cannot accept false dogmas such as evolution; such as that of believing that all humanoids are perfect and complete human beings who possess their existential bodies; such as fearing the igneous serpent of our magical powers and the lived experience, etc. We prefer instead to follow the path of authentic wisdom, the path of the Tantras, the path of the dissolution of the ego and of the recognition of our own misery and incapacity. Yes, we prefer to recognize that we are nothing, that we are only miserable slugs in the mud. Yes, we are concerned about working on ourselves, upon ourselves. We want the dissolution of the "myself," of the "oneself."

We, the Gnostics, use the intelligent power of the creative energy. We work in the forge of the Cyclops, which frightens pseudo-esotericists and pseudo-occultists so much. Therefore, we are on a different, one hundred percent revolutionary path, and which nonetheless has the frightening antiquity that is lost in the unbearable night of all ages.

Certainly, the characteristics of the Kalkian personalities are unmistakable. Above all, their self-sufficiency, their terrible pride, and their frightening vanity (based upon theories) stand out. We see, for example, in the schools of psychoanalysis, parapsychology, etc., what terrible pride and self-sufficiency seize those people with true Kalkian personalities. They stand out not only in certain groups but they also appear on television, they appear in the press, on the radio, and have the entire world completely poisoned with certain types of vibrations that in esotericism are called **poisoniooskirian vibrations**.

They have complete self-sufficiency; they look at the people of the Middle Ages with disdain. They think that they are super-civilized. They believe that they have arrived at the *non plus ultra* of wisdom. Their pride is such that they plan to conquer the infinite, outer space. They laugh at what they consider to be superstitions of the medieval sages. Behold, this is what the Kalkian personality is.

But, how does one make those Kalkian personalities comprehend that they are mistaken?

It would not be sufficient to simply tell them, for they would deny it, isn't that true? Since those Kalkian personalities have mastery over reasoning and that is their combat weapon, their little battle horse. Therefore, we have to lead them to comprehend what the reasoning process is.

We have to make those self-sufficient and proud people know that Immanuel Kant, the philosopher of Konigsberg, the great German thinker, wrote a book called *The Critique of Pure Reasoning*, as well as *The Critique of Practical Reasoning*.

If we study Immanuel Kant, we will see how he deciphers us, not only in his prosyllogisms, episyllogisms, and syllogisms, but also in the manner how he analyzes the conceptual contents in the *Critique of Pure Reasoning*.

It is clear that through external sensory perceptions we inform the mind, it then elaborates its conceptual contents based precisely on the crude sensorial connections. Because of that, it is circumscribed only by the data provided by the senses. Therefore, what can the subjective reasoning know about intuitions, and about ideas *a priori,* and about that which escapes the conceptual contents, based only on external sensory perceptions? Nothing! Isn't that so?

There exists another type of reasoning that the Kalkian personality absolutely ignores. I want to emphatically refer to Objective Reasoning. Obviously, the data of the consciousness is its foundation; it is with this data that it functions.

In authentic esotericism the consciousness is called Zoostat.

Objective Reasoning was developed before the Greco-Roman period emerged. The primeval Aryans of the first sub-race of the great Aryan Root Race (which flourished in Central Asia) had developed it. The people of the second sub-race (prior to the period of the solar Rishis) possessed it. The Egyptians of the ancient dynasties of the Pharaohs, the Babylonians, the sages of Afghanistan, Turkestan, and Iraq also used it. This type of reasoning practically ended with Greek reasoning.

The Greeks were the ones who began to play with words and ended up establishing the subjective reasoning based on external sensory perceptions, thus drowning out the Objective Reasoning, eliminating it from the face of the Earth. Since then, humanity only possesses subjective reasoning, external sensory perceptions, the data provided through the five senses.

Conceptual contents are based on the sensorial connections, etc. Thus, subjective reasoning can know nothing about that which escapes the aforementioned factors. The sensualistic subjective reasoning can know nothing about what is real, the divine, about the mysteries of life and death, etc. It is ignorant of all that escapes its sphere of action, which are the five deficient physical senses.

Unquestionably, the powers of the heart do exist. These powers are those qualities that are beyond the intellect and its purely reasoning process, which the sensualistic subjective reasoning knows nothing about.

In the land of the *Vedas* there exists an old manuscript that states the following:

> *The one who meditates on the heart center will achieve control over the Vayu Tattva* (the ethereal principle of air) *and will also acquire the siddhis* (the powers of the saints.)

In these moments there comes into my memory the case of Joseph of Cupertino. They say that he elevated himself

into the air seventy times. This magical event, which happened around 1650, was the reason why he was canonized. It is indubitable that he had his heart center developed. When a Cardinal interrogated him, he asked, "Well, why is it that you clamor at the moment that you are going to rise while in prayer?"

He then answered, "The gunpowder, when ignited in the harquebus, explodes with a great noise. The same thing occurs to the heart when it is inflamed by Divine Love."

So, in a practical manner, Joseph of Cupertino gave the clue of the Jinn State. The heart center is what we have to develop in order to be able to achieve the Jinn States.

Christina, the extraordinary saint, constantly levitated. Once she died (it was believed that she was dead), they were going to bury her, then suddenly, from within the coffin, she arose, floating all the way towards the bell tower of the church.

We could continue narrating innumerable cases... For instance: the case of Francis of Assisi. A good brother, who took care of Francis, brought him food but the monk was already in levitation, floating in the atmosphere. On other occasions, the good brother could not manage to give him the food because he could not reach him; Francis of Assisi was already too high. At times he would disappear into a nearby grove.

All these mystics had the heart center developed. Not having that center developed, one cannot acquire dexterity in the Jinn States.

Ordinarily, the one who has developed the intellect suffers much in order to achieve the Jinn States, because his intellect is developed but at the expense of the energies of his cardias. Thus, by sucking the energies of his cardias, he loses the powers of his cardias. In other words, he exchanges the powers of his cardias for his intellect.

It would be preferable to not be an intellectual and instead have the powers of the cardias, isn't that true? Nevertheless, instructors must not worry. The heart center once again can be developed by cultivating superior emotions, listening to the advanced music of the great Masters, and meditation. Thus, one develops the heart center once again by becoming more mystical, more profoundly devout. This is very pleasing.

Besides my dear brothers and sisters, we must get to know, to be able to comprehend, that the human being is divided into two consciousnesses: the true and the false.

When one comes to this world, one brings within the essence all the data (which is deposited by nature) that one needs for the inner Self-realization of the Being. But, what happens? One is put into schools where one receives a false education and much advice and precepts that are futile. In the end, one creates a false consciousness. The true consciousness within, with the deposited data that one needs to follow the footsteps, to follow the path, to arrive at the liberation of the Being, remains at the bottom, sadly categorized with the name of subconsciousness. Have you ever seen anything more absurd?

We have to become sincere with ourselves, to recognize that our false consciousness is the one that they have formed for us; the one that was created with all their theories learned in elementary and secondary schools, in college, etc., and through so many other ways (such as with the examples of our elders and the prejudices of this society in which we live). Therefore, it is not the true consciousness.

We must eliminate everything that is false within us. We must completely eliminate, definitely eradicate, that false consciousness (that is based on what we have been told, on school precepts, on college lessons, etc.) so that only the true consciousness, the Superlative Consciousness of the Being, remains within us; that is what matters.

See for yourselves how these modern psychoanalysts, these famous psychiatrists, psychologists, parapsychologists, followers of hypnotists, exert themselves more and more to drown out the true consciousness of the Being, to suppress it, to eliminate it. More and more, by all means, they want to invigorate that false consciousness that we possess.

Mesmer was a marvelous man. He had a premonition that a double consciousness existed in human beings, thus he resolved to study it. He realized that a false consciousness exists as well as a real legitimate consciousness stored in our depths and that we underestimate the real legitimate consciousness. Therefore, Mesmer began to carry out experiments of magnetism that were, without a doubt, contrary to hypnology.

Poor Mesmer, he was ridiculed and criticized a lot in his time and they still continue to ridicule and criticize him to this day. Presently many texts of hypnotism begin by talking against Mesmer. Hypnotists hate him precisely because he pronounced himself against that false consciousness; he discovered that a double consciousness exists: the false and the true consciousness. Mesmer came to unmask the false consciousness before the solemn verdict of public opinion and it is clear that they almost swallowed him. This is the crude reality of facts.

Well, in order not to deviate so much from the theme, what I want to state is that inner development is only achieved by endeavoring to throw the false consciousness into the trash and by paying attention to the true consciousness, the authentic consciousness.

What is understood by false consciousness? It is that consciousness that they have formed for us from the time that we were born. It is that consciousness that was created with examples, with the precepts of all of our relatives. It is that consciousness that they formed for us in schools, and with all the social prejudices that subsist and shall subsist.

Therefore, we have to throw away all that constitutes our false consciousness in order to cause our true consciousness to emerge to the surface so that we can work with it. This shows us that in order to work psychologically, that is, in order to put the true wisdom into play, one needs to become a child, to become an infant, a baby, stripped of all theories.

Therefore, the reason I have written this chapter is so that we center ourselves; so that we recognize the position in which we are in this world; so that we understand that we, the Gnostics, do not march on the path of all those "little schools," sects and orders that are created by the Kalkian personalities. We Gnostics are different, that is all.

Contumacy

Contumacy is the insistence of pointing out an error. This is why I will never become tired of insisting that the cause of all errors is the ego, the myself. I do not care if the intellectual animals become upset because I speak against the ego; no matter what the cost might be, I will continue with contumacy.

Two great world wars have passed and the world is on the verge of a Third World War. The world is in crisis; there is misery, illness, and ignorance everywhere.

Nothing good was left for us by the two world wars. The First World War left us with terrible influenza that killed millions of people in the year 1918. The Second World War left us with a mental pest that is far worse than the pest of the First World War. We are referring to the abominable "Existentialist Philosophy" that has totally poisoned the new generations. The revolution of the dialectic proclaims itself against such philosophy.

All of us have created this social chaos in which we live, therefore together we must all work to dissolve it. Thus, by means of the teachings that I deliver in this book, we will make a better world.

Unfortunately, people only think about their egotistical "I" and say, "First, I, second, me, and third, myself!" We have already stated it and we will repeat it again: the ego sabotages the order that revolutionary psychology establishes.

If we truly and very sincerely want the revolution of the dialectic, we need the radical transformation of the individual.

Many are they who accept the necessity for a radical, total, and definitive interior change, but unfortunately, they demand stimuli and special incentives.

People like to hear that they are doing well; they like to be complimented with pats on their back; they like to be told stimulating words, etc.

Many are they who demand a beautiful verse that will serve them as an incentive. They demand some belief, some ideology, or any utopia in order to change.

There are those who demand the promise of a good job as an enticement to change. There are those who demand a good courtship or a magnificent marriage that will serve as an incentive to change.

Nobody wants to change just like that. However, they do demand a good incentive for action.

People enjoy stimuli. Wretched people, they do not want to comprehend that such stimuli are empty and superficial. Therefore, it is worth while and logical to state that stimuli are worthless.

Stimuli have never in life, nor ever in the history of the centuries, been able to provoke an effective, total, and definitive radical change within any individual.

Within every person there exists an energetic center that cannot be destroyed with the death of the physical body; this energetic center perpetuates itself in our descendants for the misfortune of the world. This energetic center is the "I," the myself, the oneself. We need with maximum, unpostponable urgency to produce a radical change within this energetic center named the "I."

Pats on our backs, beautiful words, beautiful flattery, beautiful stimuli, noble inducements, etc., will never be able to produce any radical change in that energetic center named the "I," which is within us.

If we sincerely and wholeheartedly want a radical change within that center named the "I," then we have to recognize our lamentable state of misery and interior poverty and stop being so preoccupied with ourselves, so that we could work for humanity without seeking rewards. This means abnegation, the complete forgetting of oneself, and the complete abandonment of oneself.

It is impossible to obtain a radical change within ourselves if we only think about filling our pockets with more and more money.

The "I," the myself, wants to grow, improve, evolve, interact with the great people of Earth, acquire influence, position, wealth, etc. Superficial changes in our person are worthless. They do not change anything and do not transform anyone or anything.

We need a profound change within each and every one of us. Such a change can only be carried out within the center that we carry inside, within the "I." Like a potter's cup, we need to break the egotistical center.

It is urgent to extirpate the "I" in order to induce a profound, radical, total, and definitive change within each one of us. The way we exist and the way we like to be within can only serve to make our lives bitter, as well as the lives of those around us.

The "I" wants to fill itself with honors, virtues, money, etc. The "I" wants pleasure, fame, etc. In its crazy eagerness to expand itself, it creates an egotistical society within, where only disputes, cruelties, insatiable covetousness, ambitions without limits and boundaries, wars, etc., exist.

To our misfortune, we are members of a society created by the "I." Such a society is useless, harmful, and deleterious. It is only by radically extirpating the "I" that we can integrally change ourselves and hence change the world.

If we truly want the radical extirpation of the "I," then it is urgent to have the memory still, in order for the mind to become serene. In this way we can observe ourselves calmly in order to know ourselves.

In the same manner as one who endures and contemplates a torrential rainfall, so must we contemplate ourselves.

No one in life can dissolve the "I" by seeking substitutes. For example, leaving liquor behind but replacing it with cigarettes; abandoning one woman in order to marry another; letting go of a defect to replace it with another; or leaving one school behind to attend another.

If we truly want a radical change within ourselves, then we should set aside all those things that appear positive to us, all those old habits and all those mistaken customs.

The mind is the central headquarters of the "I." Therefore, we need a change in our central headquarters in order for there to be a true revolution within each and every one of us.

It is only with absolute abnegation and comprehension of what we unfortunately are, and without stimuli or incentives of any type, that we will truly achieve the extirpation of the "I."

The States of the Ego

The states of the ego are classified in the following manner:

Stereopsychic: These are the identifying states that are intimately related with the exterior perceptions. These are received through the five senses and are connected with the world of impressions.

Neopsychic: These are the data processing states, in other words, states that properly interpret or misinterpret all the multiple situations that the intellectual animal lives. Our personality works like a bad secretary in these neopsychic states.

Archeopsychic: These are the regressive states (memory of the ego) that are found in the 49 levels of the subconsciousness. They are the memories of the past that are filed in a photographic and phonographic manner.

Blue Time or Rest Therapeutics

Upon the mysterious threshold of the Temple of Delphi, a Greek maxim existed, which was engraved in the stone and stated: HOMO NOSCE TE IPSUM, *"Man know thyself and thou shalt know the Universe and the Gods."*

In the final instance, it is obvious, evident, and clear that the study of oneself and serene reflection conclude in the quietude and in the silence of the mind.

When the mind is quiet and in silence (not only in the intellectual level, but in each and every one of the forty-nine subconscious departments) then the Newness emerges. The Essence, the consciousness, comes out of the bottle, and the awakening of the soul, the Ecstasy, the Samadhi, occurs.

The daily practice of meditation transforms us radically. People who do not work on the annihilation of the "I" are like butterflies that flutter from one school to another. They have yet to find their center of permanent gravity. Therefore, they die as failures, without ever having achieved the inner Self-realization of their Being.

The awakening of the consciousness is only possible by means of liberating ourselves from mental dualism and by emancipating ourselves from the struggle of the antitheses or from intellectual surges.

Any subconscious, infra-conscious, or unconscious submerged struggle is converted into an impediment for the liberation of the Essence (soul).

Every antithetical battle (as insignificant and unconscious as it might appear) indicates, accuses, and aims to obscure points that are ignored and unknown within the atomic infernos of the human being.

To reflect, observe, and know these infrahuman aspects, these obscure points of oneself, is indispensable in order to achieve the absolute quietude and silence of the mind.

Only in the absence of the "I" is it possible to experience and live the integral revolution and the revolution of the dialectic.

Blue time or rest therapeutics has basic rules without which it would be impossible to emancipate ourselves from the mortifying shackles of the mind. These rules are:

1. **Relaxation:** It is indispensable to relax the body for meditation; no muscle should remain with tension. It is urgent to provoke and to regulate drowsiness by will. It is evident that with the wise combination of drowsiness and meditation, that which is called illumination will be the outcome.

2. Retrospection: What are we looking for in retrospection? Due to the mechanical life that he lives in, the intellectual animal forgets the Self. Thus, he falls into fascination. He goes around with his consciousness asleep, without remembering what he did at the moment of rising from his bed, without knowing the first thoughts of the day, his actions, and the places he has been.

The objective of retrospection is the acquisition of awareness of one's behavior or actions of the past. When carrying out the retrospection, we should not put any objections to the mind; we will recall memories of past actions, from the moment of beginning the retrospection to the desired moment in our lives. We should study each memory without becoming identified with it.

3. Serene Reflection: First, before any thoughts surge, we need to become fully aware of the mood that we are in. Serenely observe our mind; pay full attention to any mental form that appears on the screen of the intellect.

It is necessary to become sentries of our own mind during any given agitated activity, and to then stop for an instant and observe it.

4. Psychoanalysis: Examine, estimate, and inquire about the origin and root of every thought, memory, affection, emotion, feeling, resentment, etc., while they emerge from within the mind.

During psychoanalysis, one must examine, evaluate, inquire, and find out the origin of, the cause of, the reason for, or the fundamental motive for each thought, memory, image, and association as they emerge from the bottom of the subconsciousness.

5. Mantralization or Koan: The objectives of this phase are:

> **a)** To mix the magical forces of mantras or koans in our inner universe.
>
> **b)** To awaken the consciousness.

c) To internally accumulate christic atoms of high voltage.

In this psychological work, the intellect must assume a psychological, receptive, integral, unitotal, complete, tranquil, and profound state. One achieves this unitotal receptive state with the koans or phrases that control the mind.

6. Superlative Analysis: Consists of an introspective knowledge of oneself. During deep meditation, introversion is indispensable.

In that state, one will work in the process of the comprehension of the "I" or defect that one wants to disintegrate. The Gnostic student will concentrate on the psychological aggregate and will maintain it on the screen of the mind. Above all, it is indispensable to be sincere with oneself.

Superlative analysis consists of two phases which are:

a) Self-exploration: To investigate within the depths of our consciousness and in the 49 levels of our subconsciousness when the defect first manifested itself in our lives, when it last manifested itself, and in which moment it has had more strength to manifest itself.

b) Self-discovery: To investigate the nourishing foods of the "I." To fraction and divide the defect in various parts and to study each part in order to get to know the kind of "I's" it originates from and the kind of "I's" that originate from it.

7. Self-judgment: To seat the defect being studied in the defendant's chair. To bring to judgment the damages it causes to the consciousness and the benefits that the annihilation of the defect being judged would bring into our life.

8. Prayer: One will supplicate (ask) the Divine Mother Kundalini, our inner and individual Mother, with much fervor. One will talk to her with frankness and introvert all the defects and faults that one has, so that She, who is the only one capable of disintegrating the "I's," will disintegrate them at their very roots.

It is pleasant and interesting to attend the meditation halls (Gnostic sanctuaries) any time one is able to do so.

It is essential to always practice meditation with closed eyes so as to avoid external sensory perceptions.

The Corpses of the Ego

In the atomic infernos, one has to disintegrate the corpses of the ego by dint of the sexual electric force. One must not wait for time to disintegrate them.

The Philosophical Stone is the precious diamond with which Solomon polished the precious stones.

Upon disintegrating the corpses of the ego, we must direct all of our efforts in not creating physical bodies again because they are vulnerable and exposed to aging and death.

Indubitably, physical bodies are created because of Karma.

People of this day and age are not profound; they rather like being superficial. They believe themselves capable of laughing at all civilizations. This is because they lack psychological work.

Presently, the human mind is degenerated due to the matter of concepts. Every concept that is emitted is the result of what others have said, of what others have studied.

Self-concept is based on the experience of one's own form of thinking.

Gurdjieff is incipient in his teachings.

Krishnamurti has self-concepts because he has never read anything written by anyone.

When self-authority is not possessed within, imbalance and rupture with the harmony of the cosmos occurs.

How can one possess self-authority if one is not lord of oneself?

Self-action can only be possible when one has the Being within.

The Philosophical Stone, self-concept, self-action, and self-authority are only possible when one disintegrates the corpses of the ego within the psychological atomic infernos.

Psychogenesis

Apparently, our civilization appears to be so brilliant because of its conquest of outer space and the penetration of matter, but in reality, it is rotten due to the leprosy of the decadent ethics of homosexuality, lesbianism, and drug addiction.

The present civilization has entered into its phase of devolution in order to terminate itself (as had occurred with other civilizations). As a testimony to this, history shows us that when the signs of devolution surged forth from within the arrogant and imperial Rome, the greatness of this austere and moral nation suffered radical changes and sunk it into vices. This occurred after having been a conquering community of the old world.

What do I base this on? On clear and conclusive facts! A great culture such as that of England now only exports a psychological leprosy that is mentally contaminating the young generations of this day and age. The British group The Sex Pistols is capable of doing everything that is contrary to what is established, but negatively. This they do in order to appear as outstanding figures. They are the creators of punk rock and fabricators of songs that are plagued with bad words and themes that they employ for direct attack of not only institutions, but also against the public itself who listens to them with a sleeping consciousness. Filth is the flag of The Sex Pistols; they deliver a subjective message, rotten to the core, to this barren humanity. Thus, The Sex Pistols is an aggressive group that commits abuses against everything that is pointed out by the punk rock religion. Songs against love, filled with cynicism and aggression, but against repression, are created by four young people of the English working class who are against elitism.

It is ludicrous that these intellectual animals are able to create a religion when ignoring that the word *religion* comes from the Greek *religare*, which means "union with the Divinity." But, what type of divinity do these degenerated people have that young people adore in their hypnotic trance, as if it was something great?

The musical current that is shown by The Sex Pistols creates the most infernal atmosphere in present existence. This is confirmed by the hundreds of young people who were at the concert at the One Hundred Club in London; they sunk themselves into the most profound spiritual and psychological ignorance.

The punk wave advances in spite of opposition, and their subjective fashion already appears in innumerable international magazines. Clothes cut into strips, discarded pieces of any existent materials that they employ as adornment. Short hair dyed with many colors, shirts and T-shirts with statements against everything. This is a clear demonstration of the symptoms of the psychological leprosy that this humanity has and that makes it so rotten.

In many of their "encounters," physical aggressiveness (anger) is a habit. With enormous ease, insults are uttered; bottles are even flung from the very stage of The Sex Pistols. Often, all of this leads to brawls, jail, and even hospitals.

As an outcome of all of this insulting verbiage and flinging of objects, hundreds of young people appear at their concerts, yelling that they love The Sex Pistols because they are "the maximum" (as had occurred at The Paradise Club on Brewer Street).

Curiously, this band is led by Johnny Rotten (the leader who had never ever sung before this), Sid Vicious, Paul Cook, and Steve Jones. They do not respect anyone in England and it would be very difficult for them to come into our country.

I consider that life could not be explained without periodic evolution and devolution (such as that of the punk wave).

This can also be noticed in plants, animals, human beings, in stars, and in constellations.

Likewise, historical cycles have their evolution and they also have their devolution, which fatally presents itself. Devolution wears out rocks, pulverizes suns, transforms someone who was once a boy into an old man, transforms the tree into coal, and sinks continents into the bottom of the oceans, or causes them to emerge.

Our postulates presented in this book seek to establish the foundations of a new civilization that will not have leprosy and that will be based on psychogenesis. In other words, it will first be based on the creation of the Man (the true human being), and it will then move towards the creation of the Superman through mental and Sexual Super-dynamics (which we have been emphasizing in this book).

Whosoever wishes to do so can enter into our Gnostic institutions (that disseminate my teachings), as long as they have aspirations to improve and to carry out the psychogenesis within themselves, here and now.

People who have not carried out the psychogenesis within themselves can only use an infinitely small part of their capacities and potential. This is why I invite our readers to practice the psychological teachings that I deliver in these chapters so that they can learn how to obtain the maximum yield from their psyche.

Within every human being there exist infinite possibilities for a limitless knowledge. All of us possess (in an embryonic stage) great psychological faculties that will emerge in that very moment when we initiate the work, that is, when we accomplish the psychogenesis within ourselves, without delay, here, in this very instant. The human being must prepare himself to know everything that concerns him within his existence. This fact is as natural as free will.

Why are we here? Where did we come from? Where are we going? All of this must be known here. Thus, we will prevail, free of dogmas and theories.

In other words, we will be able to improve psychically; we will be able to accomplish the psychogenesis in ourselves by means of the psychological disciplines that I have been indicating. Thus, we will place ourselves in contact with the different dimensions of nature.

Consequently, as we work on our psychogenesis, our own individual improvement will be perceived. This is how we will have access to the profound esoteric teachings that throughout the course of countless centuries have been there at the disposal of every human being who sincerely yearns to find an answer to a number of questions and who has an internal emptiness. Teachings that, without us knowing it, answer the immortal suggestion of the Great Master: *Seek and thou shalt find...*

In synthesis, we will say that psychogenesis is based on the phrase inscribed on the Temple of Delphi:

> *I warn thee, whosoever thou art, Oh, thou who wish to probe the arcana of nature, if thou do not find within thyself that which thou seek, neither shalt thou be able to find it outside. If thou ignore the excellencies of thy own house, how doth thou intend to find other excellencies? Within thee is hidden the treasure of treasures. Oh, man, know thyself, thus thou shalt know the universe and the Gods!*

The Transformation of Impressions

We are going to talk about the transformation of life. This transformation is only possible if one has the resolution to profoundly do it unto oneself.

Transformation signifies that one thing changes into something else. It is logical that everything is susceptible to change.

Well-known transformations within matter exist; this no one can deny. For example, sugar is transformed into alcohol and the latter is then converted into vinegar through the action of fermentation. This is the transformation of a molecular substance. One knows about the chemical life of elements, for example, when radium is slowly transformed into lead.

The alchemists of the Middle Ages spoke about the transmutation of lead into gold; nevertheless they were not always concerned with only the mere metallic physical matter. More specifically, what they wanted to indicate with such a statement was how the transmutation of the lead of the personality can be transformed into the gold of the spirit. Therefore, it is convenient for us to reflect upon all of these things.

In the Gospels, the idea of the earthly man (who is comparable to a seed that is capable of development) has the same meaning as the idea of the renaissance of the human being, or the man who has to be born again. Obviously, if the seed does not die, the plant cannot be born. Death and birth coexist in every transformation.

In Gnosis, we consider the human being to be like a factory with three floors that normally absorbs three types of nourishment.

Common nourishment, which is a matter related to the stomach, is the first type, which corresponds to the inferior floor of the factory. Naturally, air is related with the second floor and this second type of nourishment corresponds to the lungs. Indubitably, impressions are associated with the third floor or the third type of nourishment and this corresponds to the brain.

Unquestionably, the food that we eat suffers successive transformations. The process of life, in and of itself, is transformation. Each creature in the universe subsists by means of the transformation of one substance into another. For example, a plant transforms water, air, and the salts of the earth into new vital vegetable substances such as nuts, fruits, potatoes, lemons, etc., elements that are useful to us. Therefore, everything is about transformation.

The fermentations of nature vary because of the action of the solar light. Unquestionably, the sensitive film of life (which normally extends over the face of the Earth) conducts every universal force towards the very interior of the planetary world. Therefore, each plant, each insect, each creature, and the intellectual animal himself (who is mistakenly called human) unconsciously absorb, assimilate, specific cosmic energies, which are then transformed and transmitted towards the interior layers of the planetary organism. Such transformed energies are intimately related with the whole economy of the planetary organism in which we live. Indubitably, every creature (according to its species) transforms specific energies that are then transmitted into the interior of the Earth for the economy of the world. Therefore, each creature that is in existence fulfills the same function.

When we eat a food necessary for our existence, then it is indeed transformed from one phase into another, into all of those elements that are so indispensable for our existence. Which center carries out those processes of the transformation of substances within us? Obviously, it is the Instinctual Center. The wisdom of this center is very astonishing.

Digestion in itself is transformation. In other words, the food within our stomach, in the inferior part of this three story factory of our human organism, suffers a transformation. If something were to enter without going through the stomach, then the organism would not be able to assimilate its vitamin principles or its proteins. Thus, this would simply be indigestion.

As we reflect upon this subject, we comprehend the necessity of undergoing a transformation.

It is evident that physical food is transformed. However, there is something that invites us to reflect: does an educated center for the transformation of impressions exist within us?

No! Indeed, for the purpose of nature itself, it is not necessary whatsoever for the intellectual animal (mistakenly called human) to transform impressions. But a human being can transform his impressions by himself. Naturally, he has to comprehend the reason for that necessity. We state that this is performed when one possesses an in-depth knowledge.

To transform our impressions would be magnificent. However, the majority of people, as they are seen in the field of practical life, believe that this physical world will give them what they yearn for and seek. Indeed, this is a tremendous error, because life in itself enters within us, into our organism, in the form of mere impressions. Therefore, the first thing that we must comprehend is the significance of the esoteric work that is intimately related with the world of impressions.

Do we really need to transform our impressions? Truthfully, we do! This is true because one cannot really transform ones own life unless one transforms the impressions that reach the mind.

The people who read these lines must reflect on what is being stated here. We are talking about something very revolutionary, since the whole world believes that what is physical is what is real. However, if we go a little deeper, we see that what we really perceive at each instant, at each moment, are mere impressions.

If we see a person who pleases or displeases us, the first thing that we obtain from that person's character are his pleasant or unpleasant impressions, isn't that true? This we cannot deny. Therefore, life is a succession of impressions, and not a physical thing of an exclusively materialistic type, as is believed by the learned ignoramuses. Thus, the reality of life is its impressions!

Indeed, the ideas that we are enunciating here are not easy to grasp, to apprehend. Possibly there are readers who are certain that life exists just as it is and not according to their impressions. Obviously, they are so influenced by this physical world, that this is how they think.

For example: the person that we see there, seated on a chair with this or that colored suit or the person who greets us, or who smiles at us, etc., are for us, truly real. However, if we meditate profoundly on all of them, then we will arrive at the conclusion that what is real for us are the impressions. Indeed, it is because these impressions arrive at the mind through the windows of our senses.

If we did not have senses, for instance, eyes to see, ears to hear, a mouth to taste the foods (which our organism assimilates), would then that which is called the physical world exist for us? Of course not, absolutely not.

Therefore, life reaches us in the form of impressions. Precisely, it is in these impressions where the possibility of working upon ourselves exists. Before all else, what must we do? We have to comprehend the work that we must perform. How could we achieve a psychological transformation on ourselves? We do it by performing a psychological work upon the impressions that we are receiving at each instant, at each moment.

This first work receives the name of First Conscious Shock. This is related with those impressions that are everything we know of as the exterior world. What size then do true things, real people, have?

We need to transform ourselves internally each day. When we want to transform our psychological aspect, we need to work upon the impressions that enter into us.

Why do we call the work of the transformation of impressions the First Conscious Shock? It is because the "shock" is something that we cannot observe in a merely mechanical manner. This could never be done in a mechanical manner; one needs a self-conscious effort. It is clear that when one begins to comprehend this work, one begins to cease being the mechanical human being who only serves nature's purposes.

Now think about the meaning of everything that you are being taught here. If then, by means of your own efforts, you begin with the observation of yourself, you will then see that on the practical side of this esoteric work, everything is intimately related with the transformation of impressions and what is naturally the outcome of them.

The work, for instance, on negative emotions, on angry states, on identification, on self-consideration, on the successive "I's," on lying, on self-justification, on excuses, on the unconscious states in which we are in, is all related with the transformation of impressions and what results from it all.

Regarding the significance of transformation, it is advantageous to compare the work upon oneself, in a certain manner, to a dissection. Do not forget that it is necessary to form an element of change at the place of entry of the impressions.

By means of the comprehension of this work, you can accept life as work. You will then really enter into a constant state of self-remembrance. Then, the tremendous reality of the transformation of impressions will naturally reach you. Normally, or better said supra-normally, the transformed impressions themselves would lead you to a better life, depending naturally on how concerned you are with this work. Thus, the impressions would no longer act upon you as they did at the beginning of your own transformation.

But as long as you continue thinking in the same way, that is, receiving life in the same manner, it is clear that there will be no change in yourself.

To transform the impressions of life is to transform oneself. This totally new manner of thinking helps us to carry out such a transformation. This entire dissertation is exclusively based on the radical manner of transforming oneself. Thus, if one does not transform oneself, nothing is achieved.

You will comprehend, indeed, that life demands from us a continuous reaction towards it. Thus, all of these reactions form our personal life. Therefore, to change one's life is to really change one's own reactions towards it. Exterior life reaches us as mere impressions that incessantly force us to react, we would say, in a stereotypical way. If the reactions that form our personal life are all of a negative type, then our own life will be negative as well.

Life consists of a successive series of negative reactions that happen as incessant responses towards the impressions that reach the mind. Therefore, our task consists of transforming the impressions of life in such a manner that they do not provoke this type of negative response. However in order to achieve this, it is necessary to observe oneself from instant to instant, from moment to moment. Therefore, it is urgent to study one's own impressions.

We must not allow the impressions to reach us subjectively and mechanically. If we start having such control, we will begin a new life; we will begin to live more consciously. An individual cannot give himself the luxury of allowing the impressions to reach him mechanically. Thus, when one acts in this way, one transforms the impressions and then begins to live consciously.

The First Conscious Shock consists in transforming the impressions that reach us. If one manages to transform the impressions that reach one's mind at the moment of entry, then one obtains marvelous results that benefit one's existence.

One can always work on the outcome of impressions. Thus, indeed these impressions will conclude without mechanical effect, for this mechanicity is usually disastrous in the interior of our psyche.

This Gnostic esoteric work must be brought about to the point where the impressions enter. Otherwise, they are distributed to wrong places by the personality in order to evoke old reactions.

I am going to simplify this; as an example, let us use the following: If we throw a stone into a crystalline lake, impressions will then be produced in the lake and the response of those impressions produced by the stone manifest themselves in the form of waves that go from the center to the periphery.

Now, imagine the mind as a lake. Suddenly, an image of a person appears. That image, like the stone in our example above, reaches the mind. Then, the mind reacts in the form of impressions. The impressions are the outcome of the image that reaches the mind and the reactions are the responses to such impressions.

If a ball is thrown against a wall, the wall receives the impressions. Afterwards a reaction will follow, which consists of returning the ball to the one who threw it. Perhaps the ball will not be returned directly to the person, but the ball will bounce back, and that is precisely the reaction.

The world is formed by impressions; for example: the image of a table reaches our mind through the senses. We cannot say that the table has arrived or that the table has entered our cerebrum, that is absurd. However, the image of the table is indeed inside of us. Thus, our mind reacts immediately saying: this is a wooden or metal table, etc.!

Impressions that are not so pleasant also exist. For example: the words of an offender, isn't that true? Could we transform the words of an offender? No! Because words are as they are, therefore what could we do? We must transform the impressions that such words produce within us. This is possible.

The Gnostic teachings show us how to crystallize the Second Force that is Christ within us, by means of a postulate which states: **one has to receive with gladness the unpleasant manifestations of our fellow men.**

Found in the previous postulate is the way to transform the impressions that the words of an offender produce within us. Receive with gladness the unpleasant manifestations of our fellow men. This postulate will naturally lead us to the crystallization of the Second Force, Christ, within us. The practice of this postulate will cause the Christ to come and take shape within us.

If from this physical world we only know its impressions, then indeed the physical world is not as external as people believe. With just reason Immanuel Kant said, "The exterior is the interior." If the interior is what matters, we should therefore transform the interior. The impressions are interior, therefore all objects and things, everything we perceive, exists in our interior in the form of impressions.

If we do not transform impressions, nothing will change within us. Lust, covetousness, pride, hatred, etc., exist in the form of impressions within our psyche that vibrate incessantly.

The mechanical outcome of such impressions have been all of those inhuman elements that we carry within and that we have normally called "I's" which, in their conjunction, constitutes the myself, the oneself.

Let us suppose, for example, that a man sees a provocative woman and that he does not transform those impressions; the result will be that the same impressions, of a lustful type, produce in him the desire of possessing her. Such a desire is the result of the impression received, and it crystallizes, it takes shape in our psyche, and becomes one more aggregate, in other words, an inhuman element, a new type of lustful "I" that comes to add itself to the sum of inhuman elements that in their totality constitute the ego.

Anger, covetousness, lust, envy, pride, laziness, and gluttony exist within us. Why does anger exist within us? Because many impressions reached our interior and we never transformed them. The mechanical outcomes of such never-before-transformed-impressions of anger form the "I's" which exist and vibrate in our psyche and which constantly make us feel angry.

Why covetousness? Indubitably, many things have awakened covetousness within us: money, jewels, all types of material things, etc. Those things, those objects, reached us in the form of impressions. We committed the error of not having transformed those impressions into different things, such as into an attraction for beauty, or into happiness, etc. Such non-transformed impressions naturally became "I's" of covetousness which we now carry within our interior.

Why do we have lust? I have already stated that different forms of lust have reached us in the form of impressions. In other words, images of an erotic type emerged from within the interior of our mind and the reaction was lust. Naturally, there was no hesitation in the outcome of that momentum. Afterwards, new morbid "I's" were born in our psyche because we did not transform those lustful waves, that unhealthy eroticism.

That is why today we have to work on those impressions and their mechanical results which we have within our interior. Thus, within ourselves we have impressions of anger, covetousness, gluttony, pride, laziness, and lust. Within we also have the mechanical results of such impressions: a bunch of quarrelsome and wailing "I's" which we now need to comprehend and eliminate.

The master-work of our life consists in knowing how to transform the impressions and in also knowing how to eliminate the mechanical results of those impressions that were not transformed in the past.

Properly, the exterior world does not exist within us. What exist within us are impressions. Impressions are internal, and the reactions of such impressions are completely internal.

No one could say that he is seeing a tree in itself. He may be seeing the image of a tree but not the tree. As Immanuel Kant stated, the thing in itself is not seen by anyone. One sees the image of things, in other words, the impression of a tree, of something, surges forth within us, and those impressions are internal, they are of the mind.

If one does perform one's own internal modifications, there is no hesitation in the outcome of that momentum. Such outcome is the birth of new "I's" which enslave our Essence, our consciousness, intensifying even more the sleepy state in which we live.

When one truthfully comprehends that everything that exists within oneself is nothing but impressions which are related to the physical world, one also comprehends the necessity of transforming those impressions. Thus, the transformation of oneself is attained by performing such a transformation.

There is nothing that hurts more than slander or the words of an offender. If one is capable of transforming the impressions which such words produce within, those impressions have no value. In other words, they remain like a check drawn against insufficient funds. Certainly, the words of an insulter do not have any more value than that which the insulted person gives to them. Therefore, if the insulted person does not give any importance to them, I repeat, they remain like a check drawn against insufficient funds. By comprehending this, one transforms the impressions of those words. For instance, they are transformed into something different, into love, into compassion for the insulter. Naturally, this means transformation. Therefore, we need to be transforming impressions incessantly, not only the ones in the present, but also the ones of the past and of the future.

Within us there exist many impressions. We committed the error of not having transformed those impressions in the past. Many mechanical results of the same impressions exist within us; they are called "I's." Now we have to disintegrate, to annihilate them, in order for our consciousness to remain free and awake.

It is indispensable to reflect on what I am stating here. Things, people, are nothing more than impressions within ourselves, within our minds. Therefore, if we transform those impressions, we transform our life radically.

For instance: when a person feels proud because of his social position, or his money, such pride, which exists within him, has as its basis ignorance. If, however, this person realizes that his social status is made up of mere mental matter (a series of impressions which have reached his mind) and he then analyzes the value of this mental matter, he comes to realize that such a position exists only in his mind in the form of impressions. Those impressions, which money and social status produce, are nothing but the external impressions of the mind. Thus, by simply comprehending that they are only impressions of the mind, a transformation of the same impressions occurs. Then, pride, by itself, declines, collapses, and humility is born within us in a natural way.

Continuing with this study of the processes of the transformation of impressions, I will proceed with something very important. For instance, the lustful image of a person reaches our mind or surges forth within our mind. It is obvious that such an image is an impression. We could transform that lustful impression by means of comprehension. It would be enough, in that instant, for us to think that that woman will one day die and that her body will become dust in the cemetery. If within our imagination we saw her body in the process of disintegration in the grave, this would be more than enough to transform that lustful impression into chastity. Because if it is not transformed, it will be added to the legion of our "I's" of lust. Therefore, it is convenient to transform the impressions that emerge in our mind by means of comprehension.

It is highly logical that the exterior world is not as external as is normally believed. Everything that reaches us from the physical world is in our interior because these are nothing but internal impressions.

No one could put a tree, a chair, a palace or a rock into his mind. Everything reaches our mind in the form of impressions. This is it.

Thus, the impressions that come from this world (which we consider to be external) are not as external as we believe. Therefore, it is unpostponable that we transform impressions through comprehension.

If someone greets us, praises us, how could we transform the vanity which this or that flatterer provokes within us? Obviously, the praises, the flattery, are nothing but impressions which reach our mind and the mind then reacts in the form of vanity. However, if those impressions are transformed, vanity then becomes impossible.

How could the words of a flatterer be transformed? It is by means of comprehension, of course. When one really comprehends that one is nothing but an infinitesimal creature in a corner of the universe, one immediately transforms, by oneself, those impressions of praise, flattery, into something different. One converts such impressions into what they are: dust, cosmic dust, because one comprehends one's own position.

We know that the galaxy in which we live in is made up of millions of worlds. Then, what is the Earth? It is just a particle of dust within infinity. And if we were to state that we are nothing but organic microorganisms on that particle, then what? If we were to comprehend this when were flattered, we would perform a transformation of those impressions related to the praise and flattery or adulation and as a result we would not react in the form of pride.

The more we reflect upon this, the more we will see time and again the necessity of a complete transformation of impressions.

Everything that we see as external is internal. If we do not work within the interior, then we tread upon the path of error because we are not modifying our habits. If we want to be different, we need to transform ourselves integrally. We must begin by transforming impressions. Thus, sexual transformation (transmutation) surges forth within us when we transform the animal and bestial impressions into elements of devotion.

Unquestionably, this matter of impressions deserves to be analyzed clearly and precisely. The personality that we have received or have acquired grants entrance to the impressions of life. However, this personality does not transform these impressions because the personality is something practically dead.

If the impressions would impact directly upon the Essence, then it is obvious that they would be correctly transformed, because the Essence would immediately deposit them exactly in the corresponding centers of the human machine.

Personality is that term that is applied to everything that we acquire. It is clear that the personality translates impressions from all sides of life in a limited and practically stereotypical manner, according to its quality and associations.

Related to this matter, in the Gnostic esoteric work, the personality is sometimes compared to a terrible secretary who is at the front desk of an office, preoccupied with all the ideas, concepts, preconceptions, opinions and prejudices. It has many dictionaries, encyclopedias of all types, reference books, etc. Nevertheless, it is not in communication with the centers, in other words, with the mental, emotional, and the physical centers. It is not in communication with the intellectual, motor, emotional, instinctual, and sexual centers because of its unusual ideas. Consequently or as a corollary, it so happens that the personality almost always puts itself in communication with the wrong centers. This means that the impressions that arrive are sent to the wrong centers. In other words, the personality places the impressions on centers which do not correspond to them. Naturally, this produces erroneous results.

I will make the following example so that I will be better understood. Let us suppose that a woman attends to a gentleman with a lot of consideration and respect. It is clear that the impressions which the gentleman is receiving in his mind are received by the personality and the latter sends them to the wrong centers. Normally, the personality sends them to the sexual center. Therefore, this gentleman firmly believes that the lady is in love with him. Logically, it does not take long before he rushes to make amorous insinuations to her. Indubitably, if that lady has never had that type of feeling for the gentleman, she will justly feel surprised by this. This outcome would be due to a terrible transformation of impressions. Thus, here we can see just how bad a secretary the personality really is.

Unquestionably, the life of a human being depends upon this secretary, she who seeks the transformation of impressions within her reference books without ever comprehending what the event truly means. Consequently, she transmits impressions without ever taking any responsibility for what could happen. Nevertheless, the personality considers that it is accomplishing its duty. This is our internal situation.

Thus, in this allegory what is important to comprehend is how the human personality (which we acquire and which we are compelled to acquire) begins to take charge of our lives.

Unquestionably, it is useless to imagine that this happens only to certain and specific people. This happens to everyone, whoever they might be.

Through observation, one finds out that numerous characteristic reactions exist which are produced by the impressions that reach us. Unfortunately, these mechanical reactions govern us. It is clear that every person in life is governed by life itself; it does not matter if he calls himself liberal or conservative, revolutionary or Bolshevik, good or bad in any sense of the word.

It is obvious that in the presence of the impacts of the exterior world there exist reactions. Our own life is constituted by them. Therefore, based on this fact, we can emphatically state that humanity is completely mechanical.

In life, every human being has formed for himself an enormous quantity of reactions which become the practical experiences of his existence. It is clear that every action produces their reactions, which are actions of a certain type. Such reactions are called experiences.

Thus, the ability to relax the mind would be the most essential thing for us to learn in order to get to know our actions and reactions better. This "mental relaxation" (the ability to lie down in one's bed or in a comfortable arm chair in order to patiently relax all the muscles and then to empty the mind of all thoughts, desires, emotions, and memories) is magnificent. When the mind is quiet, when the mind is in silence, we can know ourselves better. In such moments of peacefulness and mental silence, we come to really experience, in a direct manner, the crude reality of all our actions in our practical life.

When the mind is in absolute repose, we can see the multitude of elements and sub-elements, actions and reactions, desires, passions, etc., as something foreign to us. These elements and sub-elements await the precise moment in which they will be able to exercise their control over us, over our personality. That is the reason why the silence and stillness of the mind is worthwhile. Obviously, the relaxation of the mind is beneficial in the most complete sense of the word, because it leads us to individual self-knowledge.

Thus, all that is life, that is to say, external life (what we see and live), is for each person his reaction to the impressions which arrive from the physical world.

It is a great mistake to think that that which is called life is a fixed, solid thing which in itself is the same for every person. Since the existing impressions related to life in the

human species are infinite, we can say, without a doubt, that
there does not exist a single person who has the same impressions as that of another.

Indeed, life is our impressions of it. Thus, it is clear that
we can transform such impressions if we resolve to do so. But
as was stated, this is an idea which is very difficult to understand or to comprehend because the hypnosis of our senses is
very powerful.

Although this might appear incredible, the fact is that
all human beings are in a state of "collective hypnosis." Such
hypnosis is produced by the residual state of the abominable
Kundabuffer organ. When the Kundabuffer organ was eliminated, what remained were the different psychic aggregates
or inhuman elements which in their conjunction constitute
the myself, the oneself. These elements and sub-elements, in
their turn, began to condition our consciousness and keep it
in a state of hypnosis. Therefore, hypnosis of a collective type
exists. The entire world is hypnotized!

The mind is bottled up within the world of the five senses.
The mind does not manage to comprehend how it could
become independent of them. The mind believes itself to be a
god.

Our internal life (the true life of thoughts and feelings)
continues to be confused by our mere reasoning and intellectual concepts. Nonetheless, at the same time, we know very
well that the place that we really live in is within our world
of thoughts and feelings. This is something that no one can
deny.

Life is our impressions and those can be transformed. We
need to learn how to transform our impressions. However, it
is not possible to transform anything within us if we continue
to be attached to the world of the five senses.

As I have stated in my *Treatise of Revolutionary Psychology*,
experience teaches us that if our Gnostic esoteric work is negative, it is due to our own fault.

It is from our sensorial point of view that we say that this
or that person of the external world (whom one sees and hears

through the eyes and ears) has to be blamed. This person in turn will say that we are the ones to blame. However, the fault, indeed, is in the impressions that we might have about people. Many times we think that a person is perverse when in reality the person is just a humble lamb.

It is very opportune to learn how to transform all the impressions which we may have of life.

We have to learn to receive with gladness the unpleasant manifestations of our fellowmen.

Mental Stomach

In the previous chapter, we learned that there exist three known types of nourishment:

1. Nourishment related with breathing.

2. Nourishment that is strictly considered comestibles.

3. And nourishment through impressions.

The outcome of respiration is the assimilation of oxygen which is so valuable for human life.

The digestion of comestibles brings upon the assimilation of the vital principles for our blood as the outcome.

The assimilation or digestion of impressions brings about as an outcome the absorption of energy that is finer than the other two.

The five senses correspond to impressions. Two types of impressions exist: pleasant and unpleasant.

The human being needs to know how to live, yet in order to do this one has to learn how to digest and to transform impressions. This is vital for comprehension.

If, indeed, we want to know how to live, then we have to transform impressions. The Hydrogen 48 is related with all the impressions that reach the mind. Unfortunately, human beings live mechanically. Human beings can transform the Hydrogen 48 into Hydrogen 24 in order to fortify the chakras. They can transform the Hydrogen 24 into Hydrogen 12 to fortify the mind and transform the Hydrogen 12 into Hydrogen 6 in order to fortify willpower.

In this day and age, one needs to transform the mind, to move it onto a new mental level. Otherwise, impressions will always continue to arrive in the wrong centers. People believe that they are able to see things from different angles and that they are almighty. However, they do not realize that their human mind is limited by their preconceptions and prejudices.

In these modern times, we need to transform our mental apparatus; we must be different, distinct. It is urgent and necessary to build a superior intellectual apparatus that will be adequate in order to transform and digest impressions.

In the same manner that the digestive apparatus has a stomach in order to assimilate the food, in the same manner that the respiratory system has lungs to assimilate oxygen, so too must a mental stomach be created by the mechanical human being. Please do not misunderstand or misinterpret this statement. This is not a bodily cellular stomach.

We have to transform impressions before digesting them. The creation of such a mental stomach is granted and facilitated by the Gnostic teachings, consequently making the intellectual animal something different.

The necessity of transformation cannot be born without having comprehended such a necessity. This comprehension emerges when one has the Gnostic knowledge.

When one thinks differently and positively about people, it is a sign that one is changing. We need to cease being what we are in order to become what we are not. One has to become missing to oneself. The outcome of all of this is the advent of someone who is not oneself.

On the path of the transformation of impressions, we have to be sincere with ourselves and we do not have to persuade ourselves. Justification appears in us in the beginning; however we need to study that such a justification might be the fruit of self-esteem.

We need to discover the causes and motives of our behavior while in the presence of impressions. When impressions are transformed, everything becomes new.

Only the Masters of the Occult Fraternity can immediately transform their impressions, whereas human machines do not transform them.

Those situations which were brought about through past, present and future impressions can only be modified by a conscious human being. Therefore, if people will not be capable of transforming their circumstances, they will continue being toys of circumstances and of others.

Life has an objective. A superior world is the objective of life. Thus, the Gnostic teachings instruct us in how to live in a superior world, how to live in a solar and immortal humanity; if one would not accept a superior world, transformation would then not have a purpose, this is obvious.

As it is now, our mind is good for nothing. One needs to organize it, remodel it, furnish it, etc., in other words, to place it on a superior intellectual level.

In order to be able to transform our impressions, we need to reconstruct the scene just as it happened, to find out what hurt us the most. If there is no digestion of impressions, then nourishment from them will not be attained. If there is no nourishment, the essential bodies of the Being will languish.

The "I" is governed and nourished with the Hydrogen 48. Each day, each hour, new "I's" are continuously being born. For instance: mosquitoes bother us, the rain also, etc. Therefore, an addition and subtraction of "I's" always exist.

Good impressions should also be transformed. If during the day one has had three impressions which have affected his psychological mood, then they must be studied and transformed at night by utilizing an orderly procedure. Each "I" is connected with others; they are associated. The "I's" conjoin together in order to form the same scene.

We have to be analytical and judicious in order to transform impressions, so that new faculties will appear as an outcome. When people do not transform themselves, they continue to have a shameful and ludicrous psychological state. One is devolving if the digestion of impressions does not exist.

Therefore, we have to digest the impressions the same day... Do not permit the sun to set on your anger! We have to see things as they are. We have to create the convenient mental apparatus or the mental stomach in order to not become victims of anything.

The System for the Transformation of the Impressions of the Day

1. Absolute relaxation.
2. Reach the state of meditation.
3. Relive the scene just as it occurred.
4. Seek within oneself the "I" that caused the problem.
5. By observing serenely, one places the ego in the defendant's chair and one then proceeds with the judgment.
6. Ask the Divine Mother Kundalini for the disintegration of the "I"-problem.

"Deep within, all of us human beings are narcissists.
We are in love with ourselves. Just observe a singer on
the stage: he is madly in love with himself, he adores
and idolizes himself. Thus, when applause pours
on him, he reaches the climax of his self-adoration
since that is precisely what he wants, what he aspires
to. That is what he awaits with infinite thirst.
Indeed, vanity is the living manifestation of self-esteem.
The "I" adorns itself in order for others to adore it."

A WOMAN BEFORE A MIRROR BY ANTON EINSLE (1801-1871)

Chapter II

Image, Values, and Identity

In Mental Dynamics we need to know something about how and why the mind functions.

In Mental Dynamics it is urgent to know something about the how and why of the different functionalisms of the mind.

A realistic system is needed if we truly want to know the potential of the human mind.

We need to improve the quality of values, identity and image of ourselves. I think that a change in values, image and identity is fundamental.

The intellectual animal, mistakenly called human, has educated himself to deny his authentic identity, values and image.

It is an absurdity to accept the negative culture that is subjectively installed in our mind, in our interior, and follow the path of least resistance. We need an objective culture.

Unquestionably, it is an absurdity to just accept the subjective culture of this decadent age by following the line of least resistance.

We need to undergo a total revolution and a definitive change in this matter of image, values and identity.

The exterior image of a human being and the diverse circumstances that surround him are the exact result of his interior image and of his psychological processes.

Self-image is different; it is the inner K-H, the Kosmic Human, the Kosmos Human, our divine prototype, the Real Being.

Image, values and identity must be changed radically. This is Integral Revolution. We need the identity of the Being, the values of the Being, and the image of the Being.

If we discover the reserves of intelligence contained in the mind, we can liberate it.

The reserves of intelligence are the different parts of the Being that orient us in the work related with the disintegration of the ego and with the liberation of the mind.

The reserves of intelligence contained in the mind orient us in the work related with the liberation of the mind. The values of the Being constitute the intelligence. The reserves of intelligence are the diverse parts of the Being that guide and orient us in the psychological work related to the annihilation of the ego and the liberation of the mind.

Let us always make a differentiation between mind and Being. When someone accepts that the mind is bottled up within the ego, it indicates that he has begun to mature.

In the matter of the dissolution of the ego, it is necessary to combine structural and transactional analysis.

Only the values of intelligence can liberate the mind by means of the disintegration of the undesirable psychic elements.

Self-criticism

We must be sincere with ourselves by performing a dissection of our "I" with the tremendous scalpel of "self-criticism." It is an absurdity to criticize the errors of others. What is fundamental is to discover our own errors and to then disintegrate them on the basis of analysis and profound comprehension.

It is only possible to act collectively when each individual is capable of acting individually with complete and absolute consciousness of what is being done.

The systems of the revolution of the dialectic will seem very lengthy to impatient people. However, there exists no other way.

Those who want fast and immediate change in psychological and social order are the ones who create rigid norms, dictatorships of the mind. They do not yearn for others to know how to think; instead they dictate what has to be thought.

Every abrupt change defrauds its own objective and the human being becomes a victim once again of that which he struggled against. All the causes of failure of any organization exist here within ourselves.

Self-image

This matter of identifying, imagining and valuing oneself correctly must not be confused with the marvelous doctrine of non-identification.

We need to re-educate ourselves instead of retaining in our mind an obsolete and degenerated culture.

We need to have an exact concept of ourselves. Each person has a false concept about himself.

To reencounter our own selves, to correctly self-know, re-self-educate and re-self-evaluate ourselves is unpostponable.

The mind bottled up within the ego ignores the authentic values of the Being. How could the mind recognize that which it has never known?

Mental freedom is only possible by liberating the mind.

The false concepts of self-identity bottle up the mind. The exterior is merely the reflection of the interior.

The image of a person gives origin to his exterior image. The exterior is the mirror where the interior is reflected. Any person is the result of his own mental processes.

The human being must self-explore his own mind if he wishes to correctly self-identify, self-evaluate and self-imagine himself.

Human thoughts are 99% negative and harmful.

Self-adoration

Self-discovery, self-revelation, exists while we interact in society.

Indeed, during interaction, when the mind is in alert perception, our hidden defects flourish and leap forward. Then we see them as they are.

Deep within, all of us human beings are narcissists. We are in love with ourselves. Just observe a singer on the stage: he is madly in love with himself, he adores and idolizes himself. Thus, when applause pours on him, he reaches the climax of his self-adoration since that is precisely what he wants, what he aspires to. That is what he awaits with infinite thirst.

Indeed, vanity is the living manifestation of self-esteem. The "I" adorns itself in order for others to adore it.

The spontaneous beauty of the child disappears when the ego begins to control his personality. Then the overestimation of the beloved ego commences and the child dreams about dominating the world and becoming the most powerful person on Earth.

Self-judgment

The human being who allows that which is called self-judgment or inner-judgment to express itself in a spontaneous manner within will be guided by the voice of the consciousness. Thus, he will march on the upright path.

Every human being who is subjected to self-judgment becomes in fact, by his own right, a good citizen, a good husband, a good missionary, a good parent, etc.

In order to know our inner contradictions it is necessary to self-discover ourselves. The one who self-discovers himself can work successfully in the dissolution of the pluralized "I."

Inner contradictions are based on the plurality of the "I." The tremendous contradictions that we carry within make our lives painfully bitter. We are laborers yet we want to be the monarchs; we are soldiers yet we want to be generals. We think of acquiring our own house, and then when we have obtained it, we sell it because it bores us and we want another one.

We are not content with anything. We seek happiness in ideas, however ideas eventually pass. We seek happiness in interaction with friends who are with us today and against us tomorrow. Therefore, we see that everything is illusory.

Nothing in life can give us happiness. With so many contradictions we are miserable people.

It is necessary to terminate the pluralized "I." It is only in this manner that we can terminate the secret origin of all of our contradictions and bitterness.

Those who have already dissolved the "I" possess, in fact, the PCC.

There exist many schools and systems in the world and many people who live like butterflies, fluttering from one school to the next. They are always full of inner contradictions, always dissatisfied. They are always seeking the path yet they do not find it, even when it is in front of their eyes. Their pluralized "I" does not let them see the path of truth and life. The "I" is the worst enemy of illumination.

Once, a Master was asked, "What is the way?"

"What a magnificent mountain!" he said of the mountain where he was having his retreat.

"I did not ask you about the mountain, but rather about the way."

"As long as you cannot go beyond the mountain, you will not be able to find the way," replied the Master.

The "I" can also do good deeds and gain many merits which improve its psychological character. Nevertheless, the "I" will never be able to reach illumination.

We must seek only illumination, for the rest will be added onto that. It is impossible to reach illumination without having the PCC.

It is impossible to have a Permanent Center of Consciousness without having dissolved the pluralized "I."

The Auto-idea

Intellectual information and other people's ideas are not living experiences. Erudition is not experimentation. The exclusively tridimensional rehearsal, test, or demonstration is not unitotal.

Opinions, concepts, theories, and hypotheses do not mean verification, or experimentation, or full consciousness about this or that phenomenon.

A faculty that is superior to the mind, that is independent of the intellect, must exist, a faculty capable of giving us direct experience and knowledge about any phenomenon.

Only by liberating ourselves from the mind can we truly experience that which is real, that which exists in a potential state behind any phenomenon.

The world is nothing more than an illusory mental form that will inevitably dissolve at the end of the Great Cosmic Day.

Myself, my body, my friends, my things, my family, etc., are in the end that which the Hindus call "Maya," illusion. They are vain mental forms that sooner or later will be reduced to cosmic dust.

My affections, the most beloved beings which surround me, etc., are simple forms of the cosmic mind. They do not have a real existence.

Intellectual dualism, such as pleasure and pain, praises and insults, victory and defeat, wealth and misery, constitute the painful mechanicity of the mind.

Auto-idea and true happiness cannot exist within us as long as we are slaves of the mind.

No one can develop the auto-idea and true happiness as long as he is a slave of the mind. That which is Real is not a matter of textual assumptions or other people's ideas, but rather of direct experience.

Whosoever liberates himself from the intellect can feel and experience an element that transforms radically.

When we liberate ourselves from the mind, the mind then becomes a ductile, elastic, useful vehicle through which we can express ourselves.

Superior logic invites us to think that to emancipate oneself from the mind, to terminate with the automatism, is in fact equivalent to the awakening of the consciousness.

But let us get to the facts: who or what is it that must get away from others' mortifying ideas? It is obvious to answer these questions by saying: the consciousness (that which is part of the Soul in us) is what can and must be liberated.

Ideas from people of pseudo-literature only serve us in order to make our existence bitter. Authentic happiness is only possible when we emancipate ourselves from the intellect.

However, we must recognize that there exists a major inconvenience for that longed for liberation of the consciousness. I want to refer to the tremendous battle of the antitheses.

Unfortunately, the Essence or consciousness lives bottled up within the exaggerated intellective dualism of the opposites: yes and no, good and evil, tall and short, mine and yours, pleasure and displeasure, joy and woe, etc.

By all means it becomes intelligent to comprehend in depth that when the tempest of borrowed ideas in the ocean of the mind ceases and the struggle of the opposites terminates, the Essence escapes and submerges itself into That which is Real. Then the auto-idea, the seed-idea, emanates with all its splendor.

Chapter III
Mo-Chao

Mo: SILENT,
SERENE.

The Chinese word *Mo* means "silent or serene." *Chao* means "to reflect or to observe." Mo-Chao, therefore, can be translated as "serene reflection" or "serene observation."

To achieve absolute mental silence in all the levels of the subconsciousness is what is the most difficult, laborious and arduous task.

It is not enough to reach stillness and silence in the mere superficial intellectual level or in a few subconscious departments, because the Essence continues bottled up within the submerged, infraconscious and unconscious dualism.

A blank mind is something exceedingly superficial, hollow and intellectual. What we need is serene reflection if indeed we want to achieve the absolute stillness and silence of the mind.

Nonetheless, it is clear to comprehend that in pure Gnosticism the terms serenity and reflection have much more profound definitions and hence these must be comprehended within their special connotations.

The feeling of serenity transcends that which is normally understood by calm or tranquillity; it implies a superlative state which is beyond reasoning, desires, contradictions, and words. Serenity designates a situation which is beyond mundane noise.

Likewise, the meaning of reflection is beyond that which is understood as contemplation of a problem or idea. Now, it does not imply mental activity or contemplative thinking, but rather a kind of clear and reflective objective consciousness, always enlightened in its own experience.

Therefore, "serene," in this context, is that serenity of non-thinking and "reflection" signifies intense and clear consciousness.

Thus, "serene reflection" is clear consciousness within the tranquility of non-thinking.

Perfect serenity reigns when true profound enlightenment is achieved.

Dispersed Mind and Integral Mind

In Mental Dynamics, it is urgent to know how and why the mind functions. We can make of the mind a useful instrument only by resolving that how and why.

Intellectual liberty is only possible on the basis of understanding, comprehension, and knowledge of the different functions of the mind.

Only by knowing the diverse mechanisms of the mind is how we liberate ourselves from it. This is how we make of the mind a useful instrument.

If indeed we want to control our own mind in an integral manner, it is unpostponable to know ourselves.

Hippocrates, the great physician, was one of the classical masters of the mind.

The human mind is conditioned.

Willpower without chains is only possible by dissolving the ego. The mind must become an obedient mechanism to the human being. Maturity begins when we accept the reality that the human mind is conditioned.

It is possible to achieve the liberation of the mind if we discover the intelligence which it possesses. We need an integral mind instead of a dispersed mind.

The Revolution of Meditation

The technique of meditation permits us to arrive at the heights of illumination and the revolution of the dialectic.

We must distinguish between a mind that is still and a mind that is stilled by force.

When the mind is stilled by force, it is really not still. It is gagged by violence and in the deeper levels of understanding there exists an entire tempest.

When the mind is violently silenced, it is really not in silence. Deep within, it clamours, it shouts, it is in despair.

It is necessary to put an end to the modifications of the thinking system during meditation. When the thinking system remains under our control, illumination comes to us spontaneously.

Mental control permits us to destroy the shackles created by the mind. To achieve the stillness and silence of the mind, it is necessary to know how to live from instant to instant, to know how to take advantage of each moment, to not live the moment in doses.

Take everything from each moment because each moment is a child of Gnosis; each moment is absolute, alive and significant. Momentariness is a special characteristic of the Gnostics. We love the philosophy of momentariness.

Master Ummom said to his disciples, "If you walk, walk; if you sit, sit; but do not vacillate."

To commence with the study of the technique of meditation is to enter into the antechamber of the divine peace that surpasses all knowledge.

The most elevated form of thinking is non-thinking. When one achieves the stillness and silence of the mind, the "I" with all its passions, dens, appetites, fears, affections, etc. becomes absent.

It is only in the absence of the "I," in the absence of the mind, that the Buddhadatu can awaken to unite with the Inner Self and take us to ecstasy.

The Subud school of black magic states that the Monad or the Great Reality will penetrate within him who does not possess the existential bodies of the Being. This is a false statement.

Evil entities are what enter into those tenebrous fanatics of Subud; evil entities that express themselves through these people with gestures, actions, bestial, and absurd words. Such people are possessed by the tenebrous ones.

The stillness and silence of the mind has a single objective: to liberate the Essence from the mind, so that when fused with the Monad or Inner Self, it (the Essence) can experience that which we call the truth.

During ecstasy and in the absence of the "I," the Essence can live freely experiencing the truth within the World of the Mist of Fire.

When the mind is in a passive and receptive state, absolutely still and in silence, the Essence or Buddhadatu is liberated from the mind, and the ecstasy arrives.

The Essence is always bottled up in the battle of the opposites, but when the battling ends and the silence is absolute, then the bottle is broken into pieces and the Essence remains free.

When we practice meditation, our mind is assaulted by many memories, desires, passions, preoccupations, etc.

We must avoid the conflict between attention and distraction. A conflict exists between attention and distraction when we combat those assailants of the mind. The "I" is the projector of such mental assailants. Where there is conflict, stillness and silence cannot exist.

We must nullify the projector through self-observation and comprehension. Examine each image, each memory, and each thought that comes to the mind. Remember that every thought has two poles: positive and negative.

Two aspects of the same thing are entering and leaving. The dining room and the washroom, tall and short, pleasant and unpleasant, etc. are always two poles of the same thing.

Examine the two poles of each mental form that comes to the mind. Remember that only through the study of these polarities can one arrive at a synthesis.

Every mental form can be eliminated through its synthesis. Example: the memory of a fiancée assaults us. Is she beautiful? Let us think that beauty is the opposite of ugliness and that if in her youth she is beautiful, in her old age she will be ugly. The synthesis: it is not worthwhile to think about her; she is an illusion, a flower that will inevitably wither.

In India, this self-observation and study of our psyche is properly called pratyahara.

Bird-like thoughts should pass through the space of our own mind in a successive parade, but without leaving any trace behind.

The infinite procession of thoughts projected by the "I" is exhausted in the end, and then the mind remains still and in silence.

A great Self-realized Master said:

"Only when the projector, in other words, the "I," is completely absent, will the silence (which is not a product of the mind) then befall. This silence is inexhaustible; it is not of time, and it is immeasurable. It is only then, when THAT which is, arrives."

This whole technique is summarized in two principles:

1. Profound reflection

2. Tremendous serenity

This technique of meditation with its non-thinking puts to work the most central part of the mind, the one that produces the ecstasy.

Remember that the central part of the mind is that which is called Buddhadatu, the Essence, the consciousness.

When the Buddhadatu awakens we remain illuminated. We need to awaken the Buddhadatu, the consciousness.

The Gnostic student can practice meditation seated in the Western or Oriental style.

It is advisable to practice with the eyes closed to avoid the distractions of the exterior world.

It is also convenient to relax the body carefully, thus avoiding any tension in the muscles.

The Buddhadatu, the Essence, is the psychic material, the inner Buddhist principle, the spiritual material or raw matter which will eventually give shape to the Soul.

The Buddhadatu is the best that we have within and awakens with profound inner meditation.

Indeed, the Buddhadatu is the only element that the wretched intellectual animal possesses in order to arrive at the experience of that which we call the truth.

The only thing that the intellectual animal can do (being unable to incarnate the Being due to the fact that he still does not possess the superior existential bodies) is to practice meditation, to self-awaken the Buddhadatu and to know the truth.

Mechanical Association

Isan sent a mirror to Master Koysen, who showed it to his monks and asked: "Is this Isan's mirror or my mirror?

"If you say that it belongs to Isan how is it that it is in my hands? If you say that it is mine, have I not received it from Isan's hands? Speak, speak, or else I will break it into pieces."

The monks were unable to pass between those two opposites and the Master broke the mirror into pieces.

Ecstasy is impossible as long as the Essence is bottled up in the opposites.

In the times of Babylon, the Bodhisattva of the most saintly Ashiata Shiemash, a great Avatar, came to the world.

The Bodhisattva was not fallen and, like every Bodhisattva, he had his superior existential bodies of the Being normally developed.

When he reached a responsible age he arrived at the Vezinian Mountain and entered a cavern.

The tradition narrates that he carried out three tremendous fasts of forty days each and accompanied by intentional and voluntary suffering.

He dedicated the first fast to prayer and meditation.

The second fast was dedicated to reviewing his entire life and his past lives.

The third fast was definitive. It was dedicated to putting an end to the mechanical association of his mind. He did not eat; he only drank water and every half hour he pulled out two hairs from his chest.

There are two types of mechanical associations which are the foundation of the opposites:

a) Mechanical association by means of ideas, words, phrases, etc;

b) Mechanical association by images, forms, things, persons, etc.

An idea is associated with another, a word with another, a phrase with another, and the battle of the opposites follows.

The memory of someone comes into our mind; this person is associated with another; an image is associated with another, a form with another and the battle of the opposites continues.

The Bodhisattva of the Avatar Ashiata Shiemash suffered the unutterable. Fasting for forty days, mortifying himself horribly... Sunk in profound inner meditation, he achieved the disassociation from the mental mechanism and his mind remained solemnly still and in an imposing silence.

The outcome was ecstasy with the incarnation of his real Being.

Ashiata Shiemash carried out a great work in Asia, founding monasteries and establishing rulers with awakened consciousness everywhere.

This Bodhisattva was able to incarnate his real Being during meditation because he already possessed the superior existential bodies of the Being.

Those who do not have the superior existential bodies of the Being cannot succeed in getting the Divinity or the Being to operate or incarnate within them. However, they are able to liberate their Essence so that it will fuse with their Being and participate in His ecstasy.

In the state of ecstasy, we can study the great mysteries of life and death.

We have to study the ritual of life and death until the Officiant (the Inner Self, the Being) arrives.

It is only in the absence of the "I" that one can experience the bliss of the Being. Only in the absence of the "I" can ecstasy be attained.

When one achieves the dissolution of the mental mechanism, then comes that which the Oriental race calls: the breaking of the bag, the eruption of the void. Then there is a shout of joy because the Essence (the Buddhadatu) has escaped from within the battle of the opposites, and it now participates in the communion of the Saints.

The Dominion of the Mind

It is clear that at each moment we have to become more and more independent from the mind. The mind is certainly a dungeon, a prison where all of us are prisoners. We need to evade that prison if indeed we want to know what liberty is; to know that liberty which does not belong to time, that liberty which is not of the mind.

First of all, we must consider the mind as something that is not of the Being. Unfortunately, people who are quite identified with their mind, say, "I am thinking," thus, they feel as if they are the mind itself.

Schools which dedicate themselves to the fortification of the mind exist. They impart courses by correspondence, teaching how to develop mental power, etc. However, all of that is an absurdity because it is not the fortification of the bars of the mental prison (within which we are captive) that is required. What is required is the destruction of those bars in order to know true liberty, which as I have already stated, is not of time.

For as long as we are in the prison of the intellect, we will never be capable of experiencing true liberty.

The mind, in itself, is a very painful prison. No one has ever been happy with the mind. Up to now, we have never known of a human being who is happy with the mind. The mind makes all creatures unhappy, the mind makes them miserable. The happiest moments that we have all had in life have always been in the absence of the mind. These have been moments that lasted for an instant, but indeed these were moments which we will not be able to forget in our lifetime. In such a moment, we have known what happiness is, despite that such a moment has only lasted for a second. Therefore, the mind does not know what happiness is; it is a prison!

We need to learn how to dominate the mind; not other peoples' minds, but one's own mind, if we want to become independent of it.

It becomes indispensable to learn how to see the mind as something that we must dominate, as something that, let us say, something that we need to tame. Let us remember the Divine Master Jesus entering into Jerusalem seated upon his donkey on Palm Sunday. That donkey is the mind which we must subdue. We must ride upon the donkey, and not allow the donkey to ride upon us. Unfortunately, people are victims

JESUS ENTERING INTO JERUSALEM

of their mind since they do not know how to ride upon the donkey. The mind is an extremely clumsy donkey which we must dominate if indeed we want to ride upon it.

We must converse with the mind while in meditation; if a doubt crosses the mind, we must then perform a dissection on that doubt. When a doubt has been properly studied, when a dissection has been performed on it, then it does not leave any trace whatsoever in our memory, it disappears. However, when a doubt persists, when we want to incessantly combat it, then a conflict is formed. Every doubt is an obstacle for meditation. It is not by rejecting doubts that we are going to eliminate them, but on the contrary, it is by performing a dissection on them in order to see that which is real, that which is concealed within them.

Any doubt which persists in the mind becomes an obstacle for meditation. Therefore, we must analyze it, disjoin it, and reduce such doubt to dust. This is not performed by fighting the doubt, but by opening it up with the scalpel of self-criticism, by carrying out a rigorous and implacable dissection on it. It is only in this manner that we will come to discover what was within that doubt which was not important, and to discover what was real and what was unreal within such doubt.

Therefore, doubts sometimes serve in order to clarify concepts. When one eliminates a doubt through rigorous analysis, when one performs a dissection on it, one discovers a truth. Thus, from such a truth, something more profound comes, more knowledge, more wisdom.

Wisdom is elaborated based on direct experimentation, on our own experimentation; it is elaborated based on profound meditation. Sometimes, I repeat, we need to converse with the mind because many times when we want the mind to be still, when we want the mind to be in silence, it persists in its stubbornness, in its useless chattering, in the struggle of the antitheses. Therefore it is necessary to interrogate the mind. Speak to the mind as follows, "Well mind, what is it that you want? Well, answer me!" Then, if the meditation is profound, a representation can emerge within us. Thus, within that representation, within that figure, within that image, is the answer.

We must then converse with the mind and make it see the reality of things, until we make it realize that its answer is erroneous; to make it realize that its preoccupations are useless and the reason why such preoccupations are useless. Thus, in the end, the mind remains still, in silence. However, if we notice that illumination does not emerge yet, that the chaotic state, the incoherent confusion with its struggle and incessant chattering still persists within us, then we have to call the mind to order once again; we have to again interrogate it, "What is it that you want? What are you looking for? Why do you not leave me in peace?" One needs to speak clearly and converse with the mind as if it was a strange individual. Certainly, the mind is a strange individual, because it is not of the Being. Therefore, we must treat the mind like a strange subject, we must recriminate it; we must scold it.

The students of advanced Zen are used to the practice of Judo. However, their psychological Judo has not been comprehended by the tourists who arrive in Japan. To see for instance the monks practicing Judo, struggling with one another, it would appear to be a mere physical exercise, but it is not. In fact, when they are practicing Judo they are hardly noticing the physical body. Certainly, their struggle is directed towards the domination of their own mind. Thus, the Judo in which they are engaged in is against each of their own minds. Therefore, the psychological Judo has as objective that is to subdue the mind, to treat the mind scientifically, technically, with the objective of subduing it.

Unfortunately, Westerners see just the shell of Judo. Of course, as always, the superficial and foolish Westerners take Judo as a practice of personal defense; they forget the principles of Zen and Ch'an. This has been truly lamentable.

Something similar has happened with the Tarot. It is known that all of the ancient wisdom is within the Tarot. It is known that all the cosmic Laws and laws of nature are within the Tarot. For instance, an individual who speaks against Sexual Magic is speaking against the Ninth Arcanum of the Tarot. Therefore, this individual is casting a horrible Karma upon himself; an individual who speaks in favor of the dogma of evolution is breaking the law related to the Tenth Arcanum of the Tarot, and so on and so forth.

THE HERMIT

The Tarot is the "measuring pattern" for everyone, as I stated in my book entitled *The Mystery of the Golden Blossom*, which I concluded stating that the authors are free to write what they please. Nonetheless, they must not forget the measuring pattern. This measuring pattern is the Tarot that is the Golden Book, if they do not want to violate the Cosmic Laws and fall under the Law of Katancia, which is superior karma.

After this short digression, I want to state that the very sacred and very sapient Tarot has become a poker game and has converted into different card games which exist in order to entertain people. People have forgotten the laws and principles of the Tarot.

The sacred pools of the ancient temples, of the temples of mysteries, have today become pools for swimmers.

The Tauromachy or the art of bullfighting (a profound science, the Taurine science of the ancient mysteries of Neptune in Atlantis) has lost its principles. Today this science has become the vulgar bullfighting circus.

Therefore, it is not strange that the Zen Ch'an Judo (whose objective is precisely to subdue one's own mind in each of its movements and stops) has degenerated, has lost its principles in the Western world and has become nothing more than something profane which is only used today for personal defense.

Let us look at the psychological aspect of Judo; the psychological Judo which the revolution of the dialectic teaches. One needs to dominate the mind; the mind has to obey; we need to recriminate it firmly in order for it to obey.

How is it possible that while we are in the practice of meditation, in those instants within which we seek stillness and silence, the mind imposes itself and does not want to be still? We need to know why it does not want to be still. Then, we need to interrogate it, to recriminate it, to whip it, to make it obey, since the mind is a stubborn, clumsy donkey which we have to dominate.

Krishnamurti has not taught this, neither has Zen nor Ch'an taught it. This discipline that I am teaching belongs to the Second Jewel of the Yellow Dragon, to the Second Jewel of Wisdom. Within the First Jewel we can include Zen, but Zen has not explained the Second Jewel, even when the prolegomena of it is within its psychological Judo.

The Second Jewel implies the discipline of the mind, dominating, whipping, scolding it. The mind is an unbearable donkey that we need to tame!

Therefore, we need to count on several factors during meditation if we wish to attain the stillness and silence of the mind. We need to study the disorder because it is only in this manner that we can establish order. We must know what in us is attentive and what in us is inattentive.

Always when we enter meditation our mind is divided into two parts: the part which pays attention, the attentive part, and the inattentive part. It is not on the attentive part that we must focus our attention on, but rather, it is precisely on that which is inattentive within us.

When we are able to comprehend in depth what is inattentive within us and study the procedures so that the inattentive becomes attentive, we will have achieved the stillness and silence of the mind. But we have to be judicious in meditation; we have to judge ourselves, to know what is inattentive in us. We need to become conscious of that which exists as inattentive within us.

When I state that we must dominate the mind, understand that the one who has to dominate the mind is the Essence, the consciousness. By awakening consciousness we have more power over the mind and thereby we become conscious of what is unconscious in us.

It is urgent and unpostponable to dominate the mind, to converse with it, to recriminate it, to whip it with the whip of willpower and make it obey. This didactic belongs to the Second Jewel of the Yellow Dragon.

My real Being, Samael Aun Weor, was reincarnated in ancient China. At that time, my name was Chou Li and I was initiated into the Order of the Yellow Dragon. Presently, I have orders to deliver the Seven Jewels of the Yellow Dragon to whosoever awakens consciousness by living the revolution of the dialectic and by achieving integral revolution.

First of all, if we truly wish to take the most advantage of the Second Jewel, then we must not become identified with the mind, because if we feel ourselves being the mind, if for instance we say, "I am reasoning! I am thinking," then we are affirming an absurdity and we are not in agreement with the Doctrine of the Yellow Dragon because the Being does not need to think, because the Being does not need to reason. The one who reasons is the mind.

The Being is the Being and the reason for the Being to be, is to be the Being itself. The Being is what is, what has always been and what shall always be. The Being is the life which throbs in each atom just as it throbs in each Sun. The one who thinks is not the Being; the one who reasons is not the Being. We do not have the entire Being incarnated, but we have a part of the Being incarnated. This part is the Essence or Buddhadatu, that part of Soul which exists within us, that is the spiritual, the psychic material. It is necessary for this living Essence to impose itself on the mind.

The one who analyzes within us are the "I's," because the "I's" are but mere forms of the mind, mental forms that we must disintegrate and reduce to cosmic dust.

Let us study something very special in these moments. There could be a case of someone that dissolves the "I's," eliminates them. It could also be the case that that someone (besides having dissolved the "I's") fabricates a Mental Body. Obviously this person will acquire intellectual individuality. Nonetheless, this person has to liberate himself even from this very same Mental Body, because the Mental Body itself (no matter how perfect it might be) also rationalizes, also thinks. But the most elevated form of thinking is non-thinking. Therefore, as long as one thinks, one is not in the most elevated form of thinking.

The Being does not need to think. He is what has always been and what will always be. Therefore, in synthesis, we must subdue the mind and interrogate it. We do not need to subdue other people's minds because that is black magic. We do not need to dominate the mind of anyone because that is witchcraft of the worst kind. What we need is to subdue our own mind and dominate it.

During meditation, I repeat, there are two parts, that which is attentive and that which is inattentive. We need to become conscious of that which is inattentive in us. Upon becoming conscious, we can evidence that the inattentive has many factors: like doubt, there are many doubts; many are the doubts which exist in the human mind. Where do those doubts come from? We see for instance atheism, materialism, and mysticism. If we tear them apart we see then that there are many forms of skepticism, many forms of atheism, and many forms of materialism. There are persons who say that they are materialistic atheists, yet they fear spells, witchcraft. They respect nature; they know how to see God within nature but in their own way. Nevertheless, when one talks to them about spiritual or religious matters, they declare themselves materialistic atheists. Thus, their atheism is formulated in a very incipient way.

Another type of materialism and atheism exists. This is the incredulous, skeptical, Marxist-Leninist type. Something is yearned for within the very bottom of this type of materialistic atheist. Indeed, this type of atheist simply wants to disappear, to not exist, to annihilate himself integrally. He does not want to know anything about the divine Monad, he hates it. Obviously, upon proceeding in this manner, he will disintegrate as he wishes, this is his choice. Therefore, he will cease to exist; he will descend into the infernal worlds, towards the center of gravity of the planet. Since his choice is to self-destruct he will perish. Nonetheless, in the end, he will continue because the Essence will be liberated. The Essence will return to new evolutions and will proceed through new devolutions. This Essence, through different cycles of manifestations, will return and will fall again and again into the same skepticism and materialism: In the long run the outcome of this conduct will appear. When? It will be on the day when all the doors will definitely close for him, when the three thousand cycles will become completed. Then, that Essence will be reabsorbed within its Monad and the latter will sequentially enter into the spiritual, universal bosom of life. Nonetheless, this will be a Monad without mastery.

So what is it that this type of Essence really wants? What does it search for in its atheism? What is its longing? Its longing is to reject mastery. Thus, rejection of mastery is what it wants within the very bottom of all of this. Therefore, it does not acquire mastery. This type of Essence does not develop its spiritual values and finally ends up just as a divine spark but without mastery.

The forms of skepticism are varied. There are people who call themselves Catholic, Apostolic, and Romanic. Nevertheless, in their expositions they are crudely materialistic and atheists. Despite this, they go to Mass every Sunday, they take the Holy Communion, and confess their sins. Therefore, this is another kind of skepticism.

If we analyze all forms of skepticism and materialism that have been, are, and will be, we discover that a sole skepticism does not exist, that a sole materialism does not exist. The reality is that millions of forms of skepticism and materialism exist. They are millions simply because all of them are mental, they are things of the mind. In other words, skepticism and materialism are from the mind and are not from the Being.

When someone has gone beyond the mind, he has made himself conscious of the truth, which is not of time. Obviously, this person cannot be a materialist or an atheist.

Whosoever has at sometime listened to the Verb, he is then beyond time, beyond the mind.

Atheism is of the mind, and belongs to the mind that is like a fan. All the forms of materialism and atheism are so many and so varied that they resemble a great fan. That which is Real is what is beyond the mind.

The atheist and materialist are ignorant. They have never listened to the Verb. They have never known the Divine Word because they have never entered into the current of sound.

Therefore, within the mind is where atheism and materialism are gestated. These are forms of the mind, illusory forms which have no reality. What is truly Real is what does not belong to the mind. That which indeed is Real is what is beyond the mind.

To become independent of the mind is important in order to know "That" which is Real, not to know it intellectually, but rather to really and truly experience it.

Thus, we can see different forms of skepticism, incredulity, doubt, etc., by paying attention to what is inattentive within us. Then when we see any type of doubt, we have to tear it to pieces, to submit it to a dissection in order to see what it truly wants. Once we have totally torn it into pieces, that doubt then disappears without leaving any mark in the mind, without leaving even the most insignificant trace in the memory.

When we observe what is inattentive in us, we also see the struggle of the antitheses within the mind. It is at this point that we have to tear apart those antitheses in order to see what truth they hold. One must also perform a dissection of the memories, the emotions, the desires, and the preoccupations which one ignores, which one does not know where from or why they come.

When within our meditation we judiciously see that the necessity of calling the mind to attention is emerging (that is a critical point where one has become weary of the mind, that the mind does not want to obey in any manner) then there is no choice but to recriminate it, to speak to it forcefully, to deal with it face to face, as we would do with a strange and inopportune subject. One has to lash it with the whip of willpower, recriminate it with harsh words until one makes the mind obey. One must converse many times with the mind so that it will understand. If it does not understand, then one has to severely call it to order.

To not identify with the mind is indispensable. One has to whip the mind, subjugate it, dominate it. If the mind continues to be violent, then we must again whip it. Thus, in this manner we come out from within the mind and reach the truth. Certainly, the truth is that which is not of time.

When we succeed to reach that which is not of time, we can then experience an element that radically transforms. Thus, a certain transforming element that is not of time exists; that element can only be experienced, I repeat, when we come out of the mind. One must struggle intensely until one succeeds to come out of the mind in order to achieve the intimate Self-realization of the Being.

We need to become independent of the mind over and over again and enter into the current of sound, the world of music. This is the world where the word of the Elohim resounds. This is where the truth certainly reigns.

Hence, while we are bottled up in the mind, what can we know about the truth? Perhaps we know what other people say about the truth. But what do we know? The important thing is not what other people say, but what we experience through ourselves. Our problem is how to get out of the mind. For this goal, in order to emancipate ourselves, we need a science, a wisdom. This science, this wisdom, is found within Gnosis.

When we think that the mind is quiet, when we believe that it is in silence, nonetheless, no divine experience comes to us it is because the mind is not quiet nor silent. Deep down, the mind continues struggling. Deep down the mind is chattering. Then we have to confront it, to converse with it, recriminate it through meditation and ask it what is it that it wants. To tell the mind for instance, "Mind, why are you not quiet? Why do you not leave me alone?" Then, the mind will give some kind of answer and we will respond to it with another explanation. This is in order to convince it; however, if the mind does not want to be convinced, then there will be no other remedy but to subjugate it by means of recrimination and the whip of willpower.

In meditation, the dominion of the mind goes beyond the struggle of the opposites. In this manner, for example, when a thought of hatred or an evil memory assault us, then one has to try to comprehend it, try to see its antithesis which is love. Thus, if there is love, why is hatred there? What is the purpose of that hatred?

For example, if the memory of a lustful act surges forth then one has to pass through the mind the sacred chalice and the sacred lance. One has to say: "Why do I have to profane the sacred with my morbid thoughts?"

If the memory of a tall person surges forth, one must then see him short and this would be correct, since the key is in the synthesis.

Therefore, to know how to always find the synthesis is beneficial, because from the thesis one has to pass on to the antithesis. Yet, the truth is not found in the antithesis or in the thesis because discussion exists in front of the thesis and the antithesis. Affirmation, negation, discussion, and solution is what is really wanted. **Affirmation** of a bad thought, **negation** of the same through the comprehension of its opposite; **discussion**, one has to discuss what it is which is real within one and within the other until one arrives at wisdom. Thus, leaving the mind quiet and in silence. This is how one must practice.

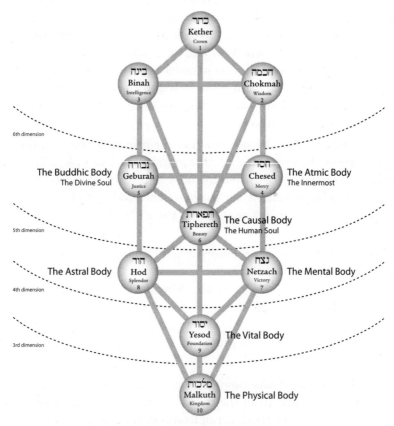

The Buddhic Body — The Divine Soul

The Atmic Body — The Innermost

The Causal Body — The Human Soul

The Astral Body

The Mental Body

The Vital Body

The Physical Body

כתר
Kether
Crown
1

בינה
Binah
Intelligence
3

חכמה
Chokmah
Wisdom
2

נבורה
Geburah
Justice
5

חסד
Chesed
Mercy
4

תפארת
Tiphereth
Beauty
6

הוד
Hod
Splendor
8

נצח
Netzach
Victory
7

יסוד
Yesod
Foundation
9

מלכות
Malkuth
Kingdom
10

6th dimension

5th dimension

4th dimension

3rd dimension

"...the mind is physical or metaphysical
matter; it is always matter. Therefore,
the mind cannot make us happy. To
know authentic happiness, true wisdom,
we must get out from within the mind
and live in the world of the Being."

All of this is part of the conscious practices related with the observation of that which is inattentive.

Nevertheless, if we simply say: it is just the memory of a tall person and we put a short person in front of it, and we finish there then this is not right. What is right would be to say: tall and short are nothing but two aspects of the same thing, however what matters is not what is tall or what is short, but what is the truth that is hidden behind all of this, because tall and short are just two illusory phenomena of the mind. Thus, this is the way in order to arrive at the synthesis and the solution.

What is inattentive in oneself is that which is formed by the subconsciousness, by that which is incoherent, by all the amount of memories that emerge from within the mind which are the memories of the past that assault one now and again, by the debris of the memory, etc.

The elements which constitute the subconsciousness must neither be accepted nor rejected. We must simply become conscious of that which is inattentive within us. Thus, in this manner that which is inattentive becomes attentive in a natural and spontaneous way. This is how the inattentive becomes attentive.

One has to make of daily life a continuous meditation. Meditation is not only that action of quieting the mind when we are at home or in the sanctuary. Meditation also encompasses the thread of daily living so that life instantaneously becomes a constant meditation.

The mind in itself is the ego. Therefore, it is urgent to destroy the ego. The outcome of its destruction is a mental substance with which the human Mental Body can be fabricated. However, this Mental Body will still be mind. Therefore, what is important is to liberate oneself from the mind. Thus, when one becomes free of it, one must learn how to function in the World of Pure Spirit without mind. One must know how to live in that current of sound that is beyond the mind and is not of time.

Ignorance is that which exists within the mind. Real wisdom is not within the mind, it is beyond the mind. The mind is ignorant, this is reason why it falls and falls into so many grave errors.

How foolish are those who make mentalistic propaganda, those who promise mental powers, those who teach others how to dominate other persons' minds, etc.

The mind has not made anyone happy. True happiness is very much beyond the mind. One cannot come to know happiness until one has become independent of the mind.

Dreams belong to the unconsciousness. When one awakens consciousness, one leaves behind dreams. Dreams are nothing but projections of the mind.

I remember a certain out of body incident that I experienced in the superior worlds. It was only an instant of carelessness. I saw how a dream came out of my mind. I was about to start dreaming, yet I reacted from within the dream that had escaped from within me for one second. Since I became aware of its process, I quickly walked away from that petrified form that escaped from within my own mind. Nevertheless, what would have happened if I would have been with my consciousness asleep? I would then have had to stay there, fascinatingly entangled in that mental form. However, when one is with his consciousness awakened, one immediately knows that in a moment of inattention a dream can escape from within. Thus, one can remain entangled all night long until the next morning.

Hence, what is important in us is to awaken our consciousness in order to stop dreaming, in order to stop thinking. This process of thinking is cosmic matter, it is of the mind. Even the Astral Body itself is nothing but the crystallization of the mental matter and the physical world is also condensed mind. Therefore, the mind is matter and it is very gross, whether it exists in a physical state or in that state called Astral or Manasic, as the Hindus state. In any case, the mind is gross and material whether in the Astral Plane or in the physical plane.

Thus, the mind is physical or metaphysical matter; it is always matter. Therefore, the mind cannot make us happy. To know authentic happiness, true wisdom, we must get out from within the mind and live in the world of the Being. This is what is important.

We do not deny the creative power of the mind. It is clear that all that exists is condensed mind. But what do we have to gain with this? Has the mind perhaps given us happiness? We can do marvels with the mind; create for ourselves many things in life.

The great inventions are condensed mind. However, these types of creations have not made us happy.

What we need is to become independent, to come out of that dungeon of matter, because the mind is matter. We have to come out of matter, live in the role of spirits, as beings, as happy creatures beyond matter. Matter does not make anyone happy. Matter is always gross even when it assumes beautiful forms.

If we search for authentic happiness, we will not find it in the matter but in the spirit. Therefore, we need to free ourselves of the mind, because true happiness comes to us when we come out of the dungeon of the mind. Again, we do not deny that the mind can be the creator of many things, of inventions, of marvels and of prodigious things. However, do any of those things give us happiness? Who is the happy one among us?

Consequently, if the mind has not given us happiness, we have to come out of the mind and find happiness somewhere else. Obviously, we will find it in the World of the Spirit. But, what we need to know is how to evade the mind, how to liberate ourselves from the mind. This is the objective of our exercises and studies which I have delivered in the Gnostic books and in this treatise *The Revolution of the Dialectic*.

Three percent of consciousness and ninety seven percent of subconsciousness exists within us. This is true. Consequently, that which we have of consciousness is what must direct itself to that which we have of unconsciousness or subconsciousness in order to recriminate the unconscious part and to make it see that it has to become conscious. But it is necessary for the conscious part to recriminate the subconscious part. This task, that is, the conscious part directing itself to the subconscious part, is a very important exercise that can be practiced at dawn. Thus, this is how the unconscious parts become conscious, little by little.

Probationism

Probationism is the science which studies the mental essences which imprison the soul. Probationism is the science of esoteric ordeals.

Probationism is that internal wisdom which permits us to study the prisons of understanding.

Probationism is the pure science which permits us to know in depth the errors of individual minds.

The human mind must be liberated from fear and appetites. The human mind must be liberated from the eagerness towards accumulation, liberated from attachments, hatreds, egotism, violence, etc.

The human mind must be liberated from the processes of reasoning which divide the mind within the battle of the antitheses.

A mind which is divided by the depressing process of options cannot serve as an instrument for the Innermost.

We must exchange the process of reasoning for the beauty of comprehension.

The process of conceptual election divides the mind, thus this is how the mind gives birth to erred action and useless effort.

Desire and appetites are obstacles for the mind. Those obstacles lead human beings to exert all kinds of errors which result in Karma.

Fear exerts over the mind the desire for security. The desire for security enslaves willpower, converting it into a prisoner of definitive self-barriers within which all human miseries are hidden.

Fear brings all types of inferiority complexes. Fear of death causes human beings to arm themselves and assassinate one another. The human being who carries a revolver at his waist is a coward; he is a fearful one. The brave one does not carry weapons because he does not fear anyone.

The fear of life, the fear of death, the fear of hunger, the fear of misery, the fear of cold and nakedness, engender all types of inferiority complexes. Fear leads human being towards violence, hatred, exploitation, etc.

The human minds live from one prison to another. Each prison is a school, a religion, an erred concept, a prejudice, a desire, an opinion, etc.

The human mind must learn how to flow seriously, in an integral manner, without the painful process of reasoning which divides the mind with its battle of the antitheses.

The mind must become like a child in order for it to be able to serve as an instrument for the Innermost.

We must always live in the present because life is just an eternal instant.

We must liberate ourselves from all types of preconceptions and desires. We must move only under the impulses of the Innermost. Covetousness, anger, lust, have their den in the mind. Covetousness, anger, lust, lead the souls towards the Avitchi.

The human being is not the mind. The mind is merely one of the four bodies of sin. When the human being becomes identified with his mind he falls into the abyss.

The mind is merely a donkey upon which we must ride in order to enter the Heavenly Jerusalem on Palm Sunday.

Therefore, when our mind besieges us with useless representations, let us talk to it in the following manner, "Mind, remove from my inner sight these representations, I do not accept these from you. You are my slave and I am your lord!"

Thus, when our mind assaults us with representations of hatred, fear, anger, cravings, covetousness, lust, etc., let us then talk to it in the following manner, "Mind, remove these things from my insight, I do not accept these from you; I am your master, I am your lord. You must obey me because you are my slave until the end of time!"

Now, we need human beings with Thelema, human beings with willpower, who do not let themselves be enslaved by their mind.

Chapter IV
The Intellect

That which one studies must be transformed into consciousness through spontaneous meditation, otherwise it destroys the intellect.

It is necessary to practice undivided, integral meditation at the hour when one feels like doing so. Meditation must not be mechanical.

It is necessary to acquire the mathematical equilibrium between the Being and Knowledge: 20 + 20 = 40; 40 - 20 = 20.

The intellectual one only sees things through his theories. Two types of intellect exist:

1. The commonly known sensual intellect.
2. The intellect which is given by the Being; this is a conscious intellect.

Degrees in the Objective Reasoning of the Being exist. These degrees are measured according to the number of tridents upon the horns of Lucifer.

It is not necessary to verbalize theories, hypotheses, and preconceptions when the interior mind is opened.

Subjective science is that which belongs to those who are enclosed in the sensual mind and who live within suppositions [read the twelfth chapter of *The Great Rebellion* by the same author].

Pure science is only within the reach of those who have the Interior Mind and among those who develop themselves amidst triangles, octagons, and squares...

Intelligence

One must not confuse intelligence with the mind. A certain sum of intelligent values exists within every mind.

We do not need to look for these intelligent values outside of ourselves because these intelligent values are within ourselves.

The intelligent values of every human being do not change, neither do they become exhausted. The reserve of intelligence is a constant.

When a positive value appears, it is in fact received happily by the intelligence.

We need a new revolutionary pedagogy whose only objective is to make us conscious of what we already know.

Identification, values, and image: to exactly identify oneself, exactly imagine oneself and exactly value oneself becomes unpostponable when we want to make an inventory of ourselves.

Enlightened Intellection

Those who manage to disintegrate the cadavers of the ego are the ones who obtain enlightened intellection.

Enlightened intellection is the intellect placed under the service of the spirit.

Jesus the Christ has enlightened intellection. He placed his intellect under the service of the spirit.

The great error of materialists consists precisely in believing that the Great Reality needs physical phenomena. Nevertheless, their "reality" after all is a product of their materialistic intellect and not of enlightened intellection.

Both the physical as well as the spiritual are energy. Therefore, the Spirit is just as real as the matter is real.

Matter is as sacred as the Spirit. To comprehend that the material and the spiritual behave in a correlated and dialectical manner will be impossible as long as the materialistic intellect does not become enlightened intellection through the revolution of the dialectic.

Time

Time is life. Therefore, whosoever does not depend on time controls life.

The flow of existence presents itself in too short a duration to allow it to transpire in trifles.

The brevity of life is enough reason to encourage us to make it greater with the integral revolution.

With intelligence we must take advantage of vital time to the maximum, in order to prolong its shortness. Let us not make it smaller with the clumsy and mean actions of the ego.

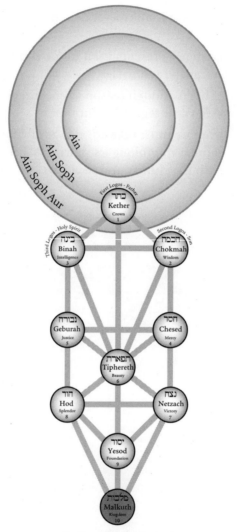

THE TREE OF LIFE: THE KABBALAH

"When we elevate ourselves to Inspired Knowledge, we
understand and comprehend that the accidental accumulation
of objects does not exist. Really, all phenomena of nature
and all objects are found intimately and organically joined
together, internally dependent upon each other and mutually
conditioning each other. Really, no phenomena of nature
can be integrally comprehended if we consider it isolated."

Chapter V
Comprehension

Within that world, which is the realm of comprehension, everything is abstract and apparently incoherent. This incoherence appears at the time one takes the first steps into the world of comprehension.

The mind and the psychological universe are found within a great chaos. This is why there is no concatenation of ideas, sentiments, etc.

In the 49 levels of the subconsciousness, a great quantity of files with powerful information exists. Unfortunately however, they are found in disorder and anarchy.

When one works in the world of comprehension, images and words emerge in the form of koans.

In the first works on the comprehension of defects, the assistance of sleepiness becomes necessary. In this comprehensive action one reaches confused levels, where images do not have coherence and where color does not yet possess neatness, in other words, color does not possess much brightness.

One of the principal obstacles in the comprehension of a defect is not being able to focus on the psychological element being studied; this is because the mind tends towards distraction.

In the world of comprehension when one tries to work on an "I," everything becomes dark; one cannot see absolutely anything and at certain moments the consciousness loses its lucidity, thus rapidly falling into fascination.

The current of thoughts and sentiments is an obstacle in order to arrive at the comprehension of a defect.

When we want to comprehend an "I," we fall into a dark void; we fall into a kind of amnesia within which we do not know what we are doing, who we are or where we are.

The force of Eros and the creative energy are the most perfect helpers for comprehension.

The creative energy, transmuted or sublimated during Sexual Magic (without the ejaculation of the entity of the semen), opens up the 49 levels of the subconsciousness, thus causing all of the "I's" (which we have hidden) to come out from within them. These psychic aggregates emerge in the form of dramas, comedies, movies, and through symbols and parables.

It is written that the clue of comprehension is found within these three psychological keys: Imagination, Inspiration, and Intuition.

Imagination

For the wise, to imagine is to see. Imagination is the translucence of the soul.

In order to attain Imagination it is important to learn how to concentrate thought on only one thing. Whosoever learns to think about only one thing makes marvels and prodigies.

The Gnostic who wants to reach Imaginative Knowledge must learn to concentrate and know how to meditate. The Gnostic must provoke drowsiness during the practice of meditation.

Meditation must be correct. The mind must be exact. Logical thought and exact concept are needed for the purpose of developing the internal senses absolutely perfectly.

The Gnostic needs a lot of patience because any act of impatience leads him towards failure.

Patience, willpower and an absolutely conscious faith are necessary on the path of the revolution of the dialectic.

On any given day, within dreams (while in meditation) a distant picture, a landscape of nature, a feature, etc. emerges. This is a sign that there is progress.

The Gnostic elevates himself little by little into Imaginative Knowledge. The Gnostic is unveiling the Veil of Isis little by little.

Whosoever awakens consciousness has reached Imaginative Knowledge. He moves into the world of symbolic images.

Those symbols that he saw while he was dreaming (when he tried to comprehend the ego during meditation) he now sees without dreaming; before he saw them with a sleeping consciousness. Now he moves himself among them with a vigilant consciousness, even when his physical body is profoundly asleep.

Inspiration

When the Gnostic reaches Imaginative Knowledge he sees the symbols but he does not understand them. He comprehends that all of nature and the ego are a living scripture that he does not know. The Gnostic then needs to elevate himself towards the Inspired Knowledge, in order to interpret the sacred symbols of great nature and the abstract language of the ego.

Inspired Knowledge grants us the power of interpreting the symbols of great nature and the confused language of the ego.

The interpretation of symbols is very delicate. Symbols must be analyzed coldly, without superstition, maliciousness, mistrust, pride, vanity, fanaticism, prejudgments, preconceptions, hatred, envy, greed, jealousy, etc. All of these factors belong to the "I."

When the "I" interferes by translating and interpreting symbols, it then alters the meaning of the secret writing and the orientation which symbolically the Being wants to give us in relation with our own internal psychological state.

Interpretation must be tremendously analytical, highly scientific, and essentially mystical. It is necessary to learn how to see and how to interpret in the absence of the loose cathexis, that is, the ego, the "myself."

It is necessary to learn how to interpret the symbols of the great nature and those of the bound cathexis in the absolute absence of the "I." Nonetheless, self-criticism must be multiplied because when the "I" of the Gnostic believes that he knows a lot he then feels himself to be infallible, omniscient, and wise, he even supposes that he sees and interprets in the absence of the "I."

There is a need to know how to interpret based upon the Law of Philosophical Analogies, on the Law of Correspondences, and on the numerical Kabbalah.

We recommend *The Mystical Kabbalah* by Dion Fortune and my book entitled *The Initiatic Path in the Arcana of Tarot and Kabbalah*; study them.

Whosoever has hatred, resentment, jealousy, envy, pride, etc., does not achieve the elevatation of himself towards Inspired Knowledge.

When we elevate ourselves to Inspired Knowledge, we understand and comprehend that the accidental accumulation of objects does not exist. Really, all phenomena of nature and all objects are found intimately and organically joined together, internally dependent upon each other and mutually conditioning each other. Really, no phenomena of nature can be integrally comprehended if we consider it isolated.

Everything is in incessant movement. Everything changes, nothing is quiet. In every object the internal struggle exists. An object is positive and negative at the same time. Quantitative transforms itself into qualitative.

Inspired Knowledge permits us to know the inner relationship between everything which is, has been, and will be.

Matter is nothing but condensed energy. The infinite modifications of energy are absolutely unknown; this is true as much for historic materialism as for dialectic materialism.

Energy is equal to mass multiplied by the velocity of the light squared. We the Gnostics separate ourselves from the antithetical struggle which exists between metaphysics and dialectical materialism. Those are the two poles of ignorance, the two antitheses of error.

We walk on another path; we are Gnostics, we consider life as a whole. The object is a point in space which serves as a vehicle to specific sums of values.

Inspired Knowledge permits us to study the intimate existent relationship between all shapes, all psychological values and nature.

Dialectic materialism does not know the values. It only studies the object. Metaphysics does not know the values or the object.

Therefore, we, the Gnostics, withdraw ourselves from these two antitheses of ignorance. We, the Gnostics, study the human being and nature integrally, seeking an integral revolution.

The Gnostic who wants to reach Inspired Knowledge must concentrate profoundly on music. *The Magic Flute* of Mozart reminds us of an Egyptian Initiation. The nine symphonies of Beethoven and many other great classical compositions like Wagner's *Parsifal* (among others) elevate us to Inspired Knowledge.

The Gnostic, profoundly concentrated on the music, must absorb himself within it, as a bee within honey, which is the product of his whole labor.

When the Gnostic has already reached Inspired Knowledge, he must then prepare himself for Intuitive Knowledge.

Intuition

The world of Intuition is the world of mathematics. The Gnostic who wants to elevate himself to the world of Intuition must be a mathematician or at least must have notions of arithmetic.

Mathematical formulas grant us Intuitive Knowledge.

If the Gnostic practices with tenacity and supreme patience, then his own internal God (bound cathexis) will teach him and instruct him in the Great Work. Thus, he will study at the feet of the Master. He will elevate himself to Intuitive Knowledge.

Imagination, Inspiration, and Intuition are the three obligatory steps of the revolution of the dialectic. Whosoever has followed these three steps of direct knowledge has achieved Supraconsciousness.

In the world of Intuition, we only find omniscience. The world of Intuition is the world of the Being. It is the world of the Innermost.

The "I," the ego, the loose cathexis, cannot enter into the world of Intuition. The world of intuition is the world of the Universal Spirit of Life.

Human Problems

The cunning and repugnant Luciferic intellect creates problems, yet it is not capable of resolving them.

Many theories exist which resolve nothing and complicate everything. The vital problems of existence continue as always. Meanwhile the world is very close to the Third World War.

The intellectual animal, falsely called a human being, feels very proud of his subjective and miserable reasoning which resolves nothing and complicates everything.

In practice, the tremendous battle of thought has demonstrated to be the least indicative to resolve problems.

In this day and age of worldly crisis, the "know it alls" who want to resolve everything (yet resolve nothing) are very abundant.

The "know-it-alls" harm the fruits of the earth with their absurd hybrids. They also infect children with their vaccines of tuberculosis, poliomyelitis, typhoid, etc. Those "know-it-alls" boast of knowing everything, yet they know nothing. They cause harm with everything that they have created and they boast of being sapient. The mind creates problems which it is not capable of resolving. The game of the mind is in bad taste.

It is true today (as it was yesterday) that the poor human biped (like a wretched and miserable simian) is nothing more than a mechanical toy that is moved about by forces which he ignores.

Any cosmic event, any sidereal catastrophe, produces certain types of waves. Thereafter, these waves are captured by the unhappy animal mistakenly called a human being; he then converts them into world wars where millions of human machines unconsciously launch themselves to the stupid task of destroying millions of other human machines.

The comic and the tragic always walk side by side. Thus, the comical things of this situation are the flags, the mottoes and all the phrases which are invented by all of those unconscious machines. They proclaim that they are going to war because they have to defend democracy, freedom, their country, etc.

The great thinkers who are known in the world as journalists (the prostitutes of intelligence) ignore that these wars are the outcome of certain cosmic waves in action and that the armies on the battlefield move like automatic puppets under the dynamic impulse of those unknown forces.

The minds of these poor intellectual animals have never resolved a fundamental problem because the intellect is the faculty which allows us to comprehend that everything is incomprehensible.

The great intellectuals have totally failed; this is being demonstrated to satiety by the catastrophic state which we are in... Mr. Intellectual, there you have your world, the chaotic and miserable world that you have created with your theories! The facts are speaking for themselves. You proud intellectuals, you have failed!

The struggle of reasoning within its intimate nature is egocentric. We need a new faculty that is not egocentric.

We need the battle to cease so that thought will remain still and serene. This is only possible by deeply comprehending the entire mechanism of subjective and miserable reasoning.

While in the serenity of thought a new faculty is born within us. The name of this faculty is Intuition. Only intuition can resolve problems.

It is obvious that if we want to develop this new faculty, we first need to comprehend in depth the complicated associative mechanism of subjective reasoning. The basic center of mechanical reasoning is the psychological "I." Such center is egotistical. This is why it can never resolve problems.

Intuition has nothing to do with that basic center of reasoning. Intuition is Christcentric.

Every problem has been created by the mind and exists as long as the mind sustains it. Every problem is a mental form which the mind sustains. Every mental form has a triple process: emergence, subsistence, and dissipation.

Every problem emerges, subsists, and then dissipates. The problem emerges because the mind creates it; it subsists as long as the mind does not forget it, and it dissipates or dissolves when the mind forgets it.

When thought ceases, beatitude is then born within us, and later, illumination comes. Before arriving at illumination we must first pass through beatitude. Three are the phases of transformation: non-thinking, beatitude, and illumination. Intuition is illumination. Every enlightened person resolves the most difficult problems.

Indeed, problems cease to exist when we forget them. We must not try to resolve problems, we must dissolve them. They are dissolved when they are forgotten. The problem is an ultra-sensible mental form with two poles, one positive and the other negative.

Do not be afraid; forget the problem. Thus, in this manner, the problem will be dissolved. Do you know how to play chess? A game of chess would not be a bad idea in order to forget the problem, or drink a cup of coffee or a good cup of tea and then go to the swimming pool and swim, or climb a mountain and laugh a little; it feels good to laugh. This will cause you to forget the problem. At any moment, a hunch comes and the problem is then resolved. Perhaps the solution is not to your liking, yet the truth is that the problem is resolved, or better said, dissolved.

A sage once stated, *"Take care of the thing before it comes into existence, therein is where any solution lies, because let us not forget that the problem has been born and has its existence within the mind."* The fact that it is raining and that you have left your umbrella at home is not a problem indeed; neither is it a problem the fact that you have debts or that you have lost your job and it is urgent for you to pay your debts. These facts are relatively true in a relative world. However, problems are something that you must kill before they are born, or solve them later, bearing in mind that the more time we allow to elapse, the greater the giant (the problem that we will have to overcome) will be.

Fear is our worst enemy. The demon of fear does not like us to resolve problems. Are you afraid that you will be thrown out on the street because you do not have money to pay the rent? Okay, might they throw you out? So what? Do you by any chance know what new doors will be opened for you? Intuition knows it and that is why the intuitive person is not afraid. Intuition dissolves problems.

Are you afraid of losing your job? Okay, you might lose it, so what? Do you by any chance know what new job there will be for you? Intuition knows it and that is why the intuitive person is not afraid.

When the battle of thought ceases, intuition is born and fear ends. Intuition dissolves problems no matter how difficult they may be.

The word swastika comes from the Sanskrit
svastika, meaning a lucky or auspicious object,
and in particular a mark made on persons
and things to denote good luck. Swastikas
are visible in archaeological evidence from
all over the world, from the Neolithic period
in the Indus Valley Civilization of the Indian
Subcontinent, to the native American cultures,
such as the Aztecs and Maya. Swastikas are
still widely used in India, in religions such
as Hinduism, Buddhism, and Jainism.

Chapter VI
A Bet with the Devil

Napoleon would have succumbed to the devil. It is one thing to be on the battlefield fighting against other males; it is quite another thing to be in a battle against oneself.

Satan is a golden enemy and he is very useful. The devil is a ladder in order to descend and it is also a ladder in order to ascend.

The Twelve Labors of Hercules are with the devil. The pact with the devil is the bet itself, and the triumph is the ability to fabricate gold.

The electric force is the cross in movement or the swastika. It is the continuous movement, the transcendent electricity which spins around like a vortex. It has served me in order to form the Gnostic Movement.

The cross in the profane and the profaners is not a swastika because the movement ends once they conclude their chemical copulation. On the contrary, in the Gnostic cross, the movement does not end because the electricity itself is transmuted continuously.

The normal duration of sexual work must be a minimum of one hour.

In India, the degree of culture is measured according to the time-span that the chemical copulation is endured. Whosoever endures three hours is respected and is a "lord."

The swastika in movement generates the transcendental sexual electricity.

Hitler understood these things. This is why he chose the swastika as the symbol of his party. However, Hitler let himself be dazzled by the "man with the green gloves" who belonged to the Drukpa clan. This man was the one who taught Hitler to crystallize everything negatively.

PADMASAMBHAVA AND CONSORT

"Man and woman, sexually united, are
surrounded by terrific cosmic forces.
Man and woman, sexually united, are
enveloped by those powerful forces which
brought the universe into existence."

When Von Litz capitulated, the monks in Lhasa (of the Drukpa clan) launched themselves upon the streets and celebrated the capitulation of Berlin.

The Second World War was a duel between the teachings of Gurdjieff and that of the Drukpas. This duel was imported from Tibet and it was a true struggle between the white and black magicians of Tibet.

Sexual Super-dynamics

To possess all the erudition of this world would be useless if one were not to die within oneself.

The destruction of the psychic aggregates is only possible in the forge of the Cyclops, in complete chemical coitus.

Man and woman, sexually united, are surrounded by terrific cosmic forces. Man and woman, sexually united, are enveloped by those powerful forces which brought the universe into existence.

Man is the positive force; the woman is the negative force. The neutral force reconciles both.

If the three forces are directed against any psychic aggregate, the latter is reduced to cosmic dust.

Man, in full chemical coitus, must help his wife by taking her psychic aggregates as if they were his own. The woman must also take the psychological aggregates of her husband as if they were hers.

In this manner, the positive, negative, and neutral forces, properly united, will be directed against any aggregate. This is the key of Sexual Super-dynamics in order to disintegrate the psychic aggregates.

Man and woman, sexually united, must pray asking Devi Kundalini to disintegrate this or that psychic aggregate (which has been previously comprehended in depth).

If the man wants to disintegrate a psychic aggregate, whether it be of hatred, lust, jealousy, etc., then he will supplicate his Divine Mother Kundalini, imploring her to disintegrate such an aggregate. His wife will help him with the same supplication, as if the aggregate were her own. The husband will also proceed in this manner with the psychic aggregates of his wife, taking them as if they were his own.

The totality of the forces of the man and the woman during the metaphysical copulation must be directed either towards the psychic aggregates of the man or towards those of the woman. In this manner we will put an end to the ego.

This is the key of Sexual Super-dynamics: the connection of the lingam-yoni (without the ejaculation of the entity of the semen) and directing the three forces against each psychic aggregate.

Let us not forget that man and woman united during the chemical coitus are truly an omnipotent and terribly divine androgen.

The Mercury

Whosoever possesses the Mercury of the wise will attain Final Liberation. To attain the Philosophical Stone would be impossible if one does not first of all get to know oneself.

The preparation of the Mercury is usually difficult. The Mercury results from the transformation of the Exohehari or Brute Azoth.

The Brute Azoth represents the sacred sperm. Many are the minerals which are transformed into Mercury. However, not all minerals can be transformed into Mercury.

The preparation of the Mercury is similar to the assimilation of food.

The Dry Mercury, the counter-transference, the ego, must be eliminated if indeed what we want is a clean and pure Mercury for the Great Work.

Twenty is the mathematical differential mean of two quantities. If the Dry Mercury is not eliminated, then the "differential mean" cannot exist.

We have to psychologically pass through the phases of earth, water, air, and fire.

One attains the refinement of the sacrament of the Church of Romae (Amore) through the elimination and psychological comprehension of the Dry Mercury.

The interior igneous rose, impregnated with Sulphur (fire) gloriously ascends through the spinal canal, thus giving us comprehension or light in order to comprehend the mechanisms of the ego.

The Mercury transforms one into a knight of life and death.

The Universal Mercury exists. The Cosmocreators had to work in the forge of the Cyclops (sex) at the beginning of the Mahamanvantara. This is not comprehended by the followers of Hegel's dialectic of nature.

Within the Chaos (mineral in a brute state) the Army of the Word, the couples, work in order to disintegrate the Dry Mercury.

A great deal of Dry Mercury had to be eliminated on the ancient Moon-Earth.

In the revolution of the dialectic, in an integral revolution, one has to perform on a small scale what the Logos did on a large scale.

The human beings who perform the Great Work, due to the fact of having eliminated the Dry Mercury from within themselves, are inwardly very different than a humanoid (although the radical differences are not noticeable externally).

The surplus of pure and clean Mercury forms a superior octave in the different existential bodies. For this purpose, one has to work in the laboratory of the Third Logos.

In order to objectively understand the revolution of the dialectic, one needs the *donum Dei*, in other words, the gift of God.

A tomorrow for the personality of the disembodied does not exist. The personality is a form of Dry Mercury in which we waste much energy. This energy is that which we must utilize in order to fortify and perform within us the transference of consciousness.

A strong Individuality totally displaces the personality, which is a grotesque form of Dry Mercury.

The energy which we spend in the personality must be utilized to eliminate everything which does not belong to the Being. Such is the case of the negative habits which are also forms of Dry Mercury.

Therefore, by disintegrating the Dry Mercury through Sexual Super-dynamics and through self-respect is how we will become accustomed to live in an impersonal manner.

Chapter VII

Fundamental Education

I will never become tired of emphasizing that the academic and educational systems of these degenerated times are useless for the authentic values of the Being. They only adulterate the authentic values of the Being.

Facts have come to demonstrate that I am right. According to the statistics of previous years, approximately 500 West German adolescents will commit suicide each school year.

It is estimated that 14,000 adolescents will try to take their lives. A high number among them (one out of every three students under 16 years of age) will have severe tension symptoms. This is caused by what the Germans denominate as *schulangst*, a word which signifies "acute scholars anxiety."

School's pressures and tensions, which some children find that they cannot endure, are responsible for one of the most critical situations which the youth must confront.

Schulangst seems to be one more social phenomenon. This is the result of a highly competitive school system, not only in Germany but also in all the countries of the world. This is mixed with high unemployment and a hierarchic society which worships foolish academic diplomas as a ticket in order to obtain highly remunerated jobs and a status symbol.

The numbers of school age children who go through this type of anxiety feel that the systems of tension are unbearable.

According to a study carried out by Karl Stritt Matter, a professor of Educational Science, one out of every three boys under the age of sixteen suffer chronic stomach problems, wet their beds while sleeping or suffer severe headaches. One out of every five students is under psychiatric treatment and it has been found that even children who are nine years old suffer from ulcers due to school tension.

What is peculiar in this matter are the statistics on school suicide, which are remarkably discouraging due to the age of the victims: among the 517 students under eighteen years of age who committed suicide in Germany in 1976, 103 were between ten and fifteen years of age. Thus the level of suicide among young people under eighteen years of age is approximately 3.3 in every 100,000 in West Germany. It is 50% higher than in the United States, where suicide among adolescents is also an alarming problem.

As long as the educational system does not operate with a fundamental education based on the solid principles of: free initiative, non-imitation, creative liberty, conscious attention, value, love, how to think, knowing how to listen, wisdom, generosity, comprehension, integration, simplicity, peace, veracity, intelligence, vocation, etc. (explained in my book *Fundamentals of Gnostic Education*) not only children and adolescents, but adults as well, will continue experiencing acute anxiety and the suicide rate will monstrously increase.

The Press

Indeed, all newspapers are filled with ideas that falsify the mind. On this path of psychological liberation it is not convenient to falsify the mind.

It is evident to me that conscious faith is necessary in order for true mental health to exist.

The press fills the mind with skepticism. Skepticism alters the equilibrium of the mind because it makes it ill.

Journalists are one hundred percent skeptical by nature.

Mental health is not possible as long as conscious faith does not exist.

The skepticism of journalists is contagious and destroys the mind.

Instead of reading foolishness, children should be taken to the countryside and fairy tales of olden times should be narrated to them. Thus, in this manner, their mind will remain open and free of the prejudices of these decadent and degenerated times.

In these decrepit and mechanical times it is necessary to recover the capacity of amazement. Unfortunately, modern people have lost this capacity.

Television

What is important in life is to not fill our mind with other people's ideas that are seen on television because with time they are converted into effigies.

The images that are seen on television reproduce themselves within the mind. These transform themselves into representations that take upon a psychological reality.

It is necessary to have the mind clean so that the Being can officiate in our psychological universe, free from the shackles of the ego.

Those who search for the integral revolution can see useful movies that are related to nature, related with palpable reality, so that they can obtain objective benefits for the superlative consciousness of the Being.

Ultramodern Music

Modern music does not have harmony or authentic melody and it lacks precise rhythm as well.

I consider modern music to be inharmonious, with strident sounds that are harmful for all the five cylinders of the human machine.

Music of an "ultramodern" type harms the nervous system and alters all the organs of the human physiology. Modern music does not keep in concordance with the melodies of the infinite.

If the ego is destroyed, one will vibrate with the cosmic music and with the music of the world of the spheres.

Romantic music is related with the things of time. It is illusory!

Classical music leads us towards the communion with the ineffable, which is not of time and which is eternal!

Solioonensius

After having profoundly studied the sunspots, the great Russian erudite Georges Lakhovsky reached the point of discovering that an intimate relationship exists between sunspots and wars.

In this era of remote-controlled rockets, profound studies have been made on cosmic rays and their influences on the living cell and organisms in general.

The complex mechanism of remote-controlled rockets can be controlled by means of radioactive waves. Neither the radioactivity of the planets in space, nor their electromagnetic influence upon living organisms can be denied any longer.

A cosmic law called Solioonensius exists. After the submersion of Atlantis, this law has manifested itself upon our planet Earth forty times. Such a cosmic law is the outcome of the electromagnetic tension of the worlds.

Our solar system of Ors has a neighboring solar system called Baleooto. In the cosmos the famous comet Solni also exists. Sometimes this comet Solni draws dangerously close to the resplendent Baleooto sun.

Many times in the past this resplendent sun has been forced to develop a strong magnetic tension in order to be able to firmly maintain its customary cosmic path. This tension naturally and logically provokes identical tension upon all the neighboring suns; among them is our sun which is called Ors.

When our sun Ors also puts itself in electromagnetic tension, (in order for the cosmic path that it follows not to be modified) it originates identical tension upon all the planets of the solar system of Ors, including our planet Earth. This is the cosmic Solioonensius. This great law acts upon our planet Earth at very long intervals.

Normally, this great law produces intense religiosity and profound yearning for inner Self-realization. However, when humanity is not psychologically prepared for the action of this law, the outcome is customarily catastrophic.

In the year 1917, the aforementioned cosmic law manifested itself intensely. Nevertheless, this Solioonensius was combined in an abnormal and negative manner within the psyche of each individual due to the fact that the Russian proletariat was full of profound resentments and bitterness. Thus, the outcome of such a negative combination was the Bolshevik Revolution.

Russia had already been preparing itself psychologically for this bloody revolution for a while. Therefore, the Bolshevik revolution was certainly the outcome of an extremely bad combination of the Solioonensius with the psychological idiosyncrasy of each individual. "Yearning for freedom" is one of the characteristics of this law when in action.

Nonetheless, during the time of the Bolshevik Revolution in Russia there were only a few people who were able to intelligently take advantage of the Solioonensius in order to develop Objective Reasoning, individual self-consciousness and the revolution of the dialectic. This will also eventually occur during these present times.

Many years have passed and we still do not know when the Solioonensius will return. What we indeed know is that we must psychologically prepare ourselves in order to receive it in an intelligent manner. Thus, with the help of the Solioonensius, we will achieve the integral revolution that I present in an objective manner in this treatise.

Therefore, it is logical to think that if the Solioonensius finds us without any psychological preparation, the outcome will be catastrophic.

It is good to record in our memory and to never forget that the Bolshevik Revolution and the Seven Day War were indeed a social catastrophe.

We must aspire to perform the revolution of the dialectic upon the Earth. It is necessary to prepare ourselves psychologically as best as possible for this objective. It would be lamentable indeed for the next Solioonensius to find us without any type of psychological preparation.

In ancient times when the Solioonensius manifested itself and humanity was not prepared it was catastrophic. Let us remember ancient Egypt; between one dynasty and another there were terrible events. Twice did the Solioonensius manifest itself in a catastrophic manner in the sunny land of Kem.

In the first Solioonensius, the people, in a bloody revolution, elected rulers through blood and death. The candidate who had within his "sacred vase" the greatest number of eyes belonging to the legitimately constituted ruling class was elected the new ruler. It is clear that the scenes of such a revolt were horrible.

In the second manifestation of this cosmic law, the infuriated Egyptian people rose against their rulers and killed them by piercing them from side to side with a sacred metallic cable. On that occasion, neither sex nor age was respected. This cable seemed more like a macabre necklace which was later dragged by beasts and thrown into the Nile.

The Solioonensius produces yearnings for liberation, for a revolution of the consciousness. However, when the human being is not prepared, the only thing that arises within him is to kill the rulers, or to assassinate others, or to dethrone kings, or cause wars, etc.

We must prepare ourselves psychologically for the Solioonensius. We need to become self-cognizant and to perform upon the face of the Earth the revolution of the dialectic.

Religious Principles

All religions are precious stones strung on the golden thread of Divinity.

All religions conserve the eternal values. False religions do not exist.

All religions are necessary; all religions fulfill their mission in life.

It is absurd to state that our neighbor's religion is useless and that only ours is authentic. If the neighbor's religion is not good then my religion is not good either because the values are always the same.

It is stupid to state that the religion of the indigenous tribes of America is idolatry because they too have the right to say that our religion is idolatry. If we laugh at them, they can also laugh at us. If we say that they adore or that they adored idols, then they too can say that we adore idols.

We cannot discredit the religion of others without discrediting ours as well because the principles are always the same. All religions have the same principles.

Under the sun, every religion is born, grows, develops, multiplies into many sects, and dies. This is how it has always been and will always be.

Religious principles never die. The religious forms can die, but the religious principles, in other words, the eternal values, can never die. They continue; they are re-dressed with new forms.

Religion is inherent to life in the same manner that humidity is to water.

There are profoundly religious people who do not belong to any religious form.

People without religion are conservative and reactionary by nature. Only religious people can achieve the revolution of the dialectic.

There is no reason that justifies religious wars like those that have occurred in Ireland. It is absurd to classify others as unfaithful, heretics, or pagans because of the simple fact that they do not belong to our religion.

The sorcerer, who in the heart of the African jungles exercises his priesthood before the tribe of cannibals, as well as the aristocratic Christian archbishop who officiates in the metropolitan cathedrals of London, Paris, or Rome, rest on the same principles. The only thing that varies is the structure of their religion.

Jesus, the Divine Rabbi of Galilee, taught all human beings the path of the Truth and the revolution of the dialectic.

The Truth was made flesh within Jesus. The Truth will become flesh within every human being who achieves Integral Revolution.

If we study religions, if we perform a comparative study of religions, we will then find the worship of Christ within all of them. The only thing that varies is the name given to Christ.

The Divine Rabbi of Galilee has the same attributes as Zeus, Apollo, Krishna, Quetzalcoatl, Lao-Tse, Fu-Xi the Chinese Christ, Buddha, etc.

One remains astonished when one carries out a comparative study of religions because all of these sacred religious personages that personify Christ are born on the 24th of December at 12 o'clock midnight.

All of these sacred personages are children of immaculate conceptions. All of them are born by the deed and grace of the Holy Spirit. All of them are born from Virgins who are immaculate before childbirth, within childbirth, and after childbirth.

The poor and unknown Hebrew woman Mary, mother of the adorable Savior Jesus the Christ, received the same attributes and cosmic powers as that of the Goddess Isis, Juno, Demeter, Ceres, Vesta, Maia, Adonia, Insobertha, Rea, Cybele, Tonantzin, etc.

All of these feminine deities always represent the Divine Mother, the Eternal Cosmic Feminine Principle.

Christ is always the child of the Divine Mother. Worship of the Divine Mother is rendered by all the holy religions.

Mary is fecundated by the Holy Spirit. Tradition narrates that the Third Logos in the shape of a dove, fecundated the immaculate womb of Mary.

The dove is always a phallic symbol. Let us remember Peristhera, nymph of the court of Venus, who was transformed into a dove by love.

Among the Chinese, the Christ is Fu-Xi, the Chinese Christ who is miraculously born by the action and grace of the Holy Spirit: While a virgin named Hoa-Se walked on the river bank, she placed her foot on the footstep of the Great Man. Immediately she was affected emotionally seeing herself surrounded by a marvelous splendor and her womb became with child. After twelve years had gone by, on the fourth day of the tenth Moon, at midnight, Fu-Xi was born. He was named Fu-Xi in the memory of the river on whose river bank he was conceived.

In Ancient Mexico, Christ is Quetzalcoatl, the Messiah and transformer of the Toltecs: One day, while Chimalmat was alone with her two sisters, a messenger from heaven appeared to her. Upon seeing him the frightened sisters died. When Chimalmat heard from the angel's mouth that she would conceive a boy, the conception of Quetzalcoatl (the Mexican Christ) took place instantly, even though Chimalmat had not been with a male.

Among the Japanese, the Christ is Amida, who by praying for all sinners intercedes before the Supreme Goddess Ten-Sic-Dai-Tain. Amida, the Japanese Christ of the Shinto Religion, is the one who has the powers to open the doors of Gokuraku - Paradise.

The German *Eddas* mention the Khristos, the God of their Theogony, who similarly to Jesus was born on the 24th of December at midnight; the same occured with Odin, Wotan and Beleno.

When one studies the Gospel of Krishna the Hindu Christ, one is astonished upon discovering the same Gospel of Jesus. However, Krishna was born many centuries before Jesus.

Devaki, the Hindu virgin, conceived Krishna by the action and grace of the Holy Spirit. The child-God Krishna was transported to the stable of Nanden and the gods and angels came to adore him. The life, passion, and death of Krishna are similar to that of Jesus.

It is worthwhile to study all religions. The comparative study of religions leads one to comprehend that all religions conserve the eternal values, that no religion is false, that all are true.

All religions talk about the soul, about Heaven, Hell, etc. The principles are always the same.

The Averno was the Hell among the Romans. The Tartarus was the Hell among the Greeks. The Avitchi is Hell among the Hindus, etc.

The Olympus was Heaven among the Romans and Greeks. Each religion has its Heaven.

When the religion of the Romans terminated, when it degenerated, the priests then became soothsayers, jugglers, etc. Nonetheless, the eternal principles did not die. Those principles were dressed with the new religious form of Christianity.

The pagan priests, denominated Augur, Druid, Flamen, Hierophant, Dionysus and Sacrificer, were re-baptized in Christianity with the sacred titles of Clergy, Pastors, Prelates, Pope, Annointed, Abbot, Theologian, etc.

The Sibyls, Vestals, Druidesses, Popesses, Deaconesses, Menades, Pythonesses, etc. in Christianity were denominated as Novices, Abbesses, Canonesses, Superior Prelates, Reverends, Sisters, and Nuns.

The Gods, Demigods, Titans, Goddesses, Sylphids, Cyclops, and Messengers of the gods of ancient religions were re-baptized with the names of Angels, Archangels, Seraphim, Powers, Virtues, Thrones, etc.

If the gods were adored in antiquity, they are also adored now, except with different names.

Religious forms change according to the historical times and the races. Each race needs its special religious form.

People need religion. People without religion are in fact totally barbarian, cruel, and pitiless.

The Fourth Unit of Reasoning

The fanatical communists mortally hate everything that contains the flavor of Divinity.

The fanatical materialists believe that they can resolve all the problems of the cosmos with their three-dimensional reasoning. What is worse in this matter is that they do not even know themselves.

The god-matter of these materialistic gentlemen does not withstand an in-depth analysis. Until now, the fanatics of Marxist dialectics have not been able to really demonstrate the existence of matter.

During the entire nineteenth and the entire twentieth centuries, the fanatical materialists have wasted their time arguing about the already tiresome subject of "matter and energy."

A great deal has been said about energy and matter. Nonetheless, in spite of all the speculations, indeed matter and energy continue being the unknown X-Y. Then what?

What is funny in this subject matter is that the reactionary henchmen of the famous "dialectical materialism" have always tried to define one with the other. It is indeed ridiculous to define the unknown with the unknown.

The poor kidnapped children of Tibet are taught in Peking phrases such as this: "Matter is that thing within which the changes which are called movements are carried out. And movements are those changes which are carried out within matter." This is the identity of the unknown, X=Y, Y=X. This is total ignorance, a vicious circle, an absurdity.

Who, at some time, has had in the palm of his hand a piece of matter without any form whatsoever? Who has known matter free of every form? Who, at some time, has known energy free from the concept of movement? Matter in itself, energy in itself, who has known these?

No one has seen "matter"; no one has seen "energy." The human being only perceives phenomena, things, forms, images, etc., but has never seen the substance of things.

The materialistic gentlemen totally ignore everything that a given substance is. Therefore, they dogmatically call this given substance "matter," whereas, what they are actually seeing is wood, copper, gold, rock, etc.

Really, the so called "matter" is a concept that is as abstract as beauty, generosity, and courage. Not a single fanatic of dialectical materialism has ever seen the substance of things in itself. They have never seen how the thing is in itself.

We do not deny that they utilize what they dogmatically call "matter." The donkey also utilizes the grass for its nourishment without knowing it, nonetheless this is not science, this is not wisdom, this is nothing. Do the fanatics of dialectical materialism want to convert all human beings into donkeys? According to what we are seeing, this is so. What else can be expected from those who do not want to know what something is in and of itself?

Art

As the human being precipitated himself downwards on the path of devolution and degeneration, as he became more and more materialistic, his senses also became deteriorated and degenerated.

It comes into our memory a school in Babylon that was dedicated to the study of everything related to the olfactory sense. They had a motto that stated, "Seek the truth in the shades of aromas obtained between the moments that something is in the act of becoming frozen and the moment that something is in the act of becoming decomposed."

That school was persecuted and destroyed by a very terrible chief. This chief had very dishonest business matters and he was soon indirectly accused by those affiliated to that school.

The sense of smell developed extraordinarily. It permitted the students of this school to discover many things which were not convenient for government officials.

There was another very important school in Babylon. This was the school of painters. The motto of this school was, "Discover and elucidate the truth, only by the tonalities which exist between white and black."

During that time, those affiliated with such a school could normally utilize, without difficulty, nearly one thousand five hundred shades of the color gray.

From the Babylonian period to these sad days in which we live, the human senses have been degenerating frighteningly due to the materialism which Marx justifies in his own manner with the cheap sophistry of his dialectic.

The "I" continues after death and perpetuates itself through our descendants. The "I" complicates itself with materialistic experiences and becomes robust at the expense of the human faculties.

As the "I" has become invigorated throughout the centuries, human faculties have been degenerating more and more each time.

Sacred dances were authentic informative books which were deliberately transmitting certain transcendental cosmic teachings.

The Whirling Dervishes do not ignore the mutually equilibrated seven temptations of living organisms.

The ancient dancers knew the seven independent parts of the body and knew very well what the seven different lines of movement are. The sacred dancers knew very well that each of the seven lines of movement possesses seven points of dynamic concentration.

The dancers of Babylon, Greece, and Egypt did not ignore that all of this crystallized in the whirling atom and on the gigantic planet that dances around its center of cosmic gravitation.

If we could invent a machine that would imitate with exactness all the movements of the seven planets of our solar system around the sun, we would then discover with amazement the secret of the Whirling Dervishes. Indeed, the Whirling Dervishes perfectly imitate all of the movements of the planets around the Sun.

The sacred dances in the times of Egypt, Babylon, Greece, etc., go even further. They transmitted tremendous cosmic, anthropogenetic, psychobiological, mathematical truths, etc.

When the first symptoms of atheism, skepticism, and materialism began to appear in Babylon, the degeneration of the five senses accelerated in a frightening manner.

It is perfectly demonstrated that we are what we think. Therefore, if we think as materialists, we degenerate and fossilize ourselves.

Karl Marx committed an unforgivable crime. He took away the spiritual values of humanity. Marxism has unleashed religious persecution. Marxism has precipitated humanity to its total degeneration.

Materialistic Marxist ideas have infiltrated everywhere, in schools and in the home, in the temple and in the office, etc.

The artists of each new generation have become true apologists of dialectical materialism. Every breath of spirituality has disappeared in ultramodern art.

Modern artists no longer know anything about the Law of Seven. They no longer know anything about the cosmic dramas. They no longer know anything about the sacred dances of the ancient mysteries.

The tenebrous ones have stolen the theatre and the stage. They have miserably profaned it. They have totally prostituted it.

The Sabbath, the day of the theatre, the day of the mysteries, was very popular in the ancient temples. Marvelous cosmic dramas were then presented.

Drama served to transmit valuable teachings to the Initiates. Different ways to experience the Being and the manifestations of the Being were transmitted to the initiates by means of drama.

Among the dramas, the most ancient one is that of the Cosmic Christ. The Initiates knew very well that each of us must become the Christ of such a drama if we indeed aspire to the Kingdom of the Superman.

The cosmic dramas are based on the Law of Seven. Certain intelligent deviations of such law were always utilized in order to transmit transcendental teachings to the neophyte.

In music it is well known that certain notes can produce happiness in the thinking (intellectual) center, other notes can produce sadness in the sensitive (emotional) center and other notes can produce religiosity in the motor center.

Indeed, the old Hierophants never ignored that integral knowledge can only be acquired through the three cerebrums. A single cerebrum cannot give complete information.

The sacred dance and the cosmic drama, wisely combined with music, served to transmit tremendous archaic teachings of a cosmogenetic, psychobiological, psychochemical, metaphysical type, etc., to the neophytes.

In addition to this, it is suitable here to mention sculpture. The latter was grandiose in bygone times. The allegorical beings chiseled on hard rock reveal to us that the ancient Masters never ignored the Law of Seven.

Let us remember the Sphinx of Giza, in Egypt. The sphinx depicts for us the four elements of nature and the four basic conditions of the Superman.

After the Second World War, existentialist philosophy and art were born. When we have seen the existentialist actors on stage, we have arrived at the conclusion that they are truly maniacal and perversely sick people.

If Marxism continues to be disseminated, then the human being will end up totally losing his five senses (which are in the process of degeneration).

It is already proven by observation and experience that the absence of spiritual values produces degeneration.

The paintings of this day and age, as well as the music, the sculptures, etc., are nothing but the product of degeneration.

The initiates of ancient times, the sacred female dancers, the true artists of ancient great times, no longer appear on the stage. Now, only sick automatons, degenerated singers, rebels without a cause, etc. appear on the stage.

Ultramodern theatres are the antithesis of the sacred theatres of the great mysteries of Egypt, Greece, India, etc.

The art of this day and age is tenebrous; it is the antithesis of Light. Modern artists are tenebrous as well.

Surrealistic and Marxist painting, ultramodern sculpture, Afro-Cuban music and the modern female dancers are the outcome of human degeneration.

The young men and women of the new generations receive by means of their three cerebrums data which is sufficient to convert them into swindlers, thieves, assassins, bandits, homosexuals, prostitutes, etc.

No one does anything to put an end to this bad art and everything marches towards a final catastrophe due to the lack of a revolution of the dialectic.

Materialistic Science

On a certain occasion, a materialistic atheist, an enemy of the Eternal Living God, had a discussion with a religious man. They were arguing in order to decide upon the following enigma: Which came first, the chicken or the egg? One of them stated: "The egg was first."

"Oh right," stated the other, "it was the egg. But who laid the egg?"

The answer: "Well, the chicken."

Then, the other one replied, "If the chicken was first, where did the chicken come from?"

The answer: "Well, from the egg." As you can see, this is a tale that never ends.

Following, the religious man, who was a little impatient, stated: "Could you create an egg the way God has done?"

The materialist answered: "Yes, I can!"

"Do it!" exclaimed the religious man.

Thus, the materialist made an egg which was identical to that of a chicken. This was an egg with its yolk, albumen and shell. Noticing this, the religious man stated: "Wonderful, since you have made an egg, now let us see if it will produce a chicken. Let us place the egg in an incubator in order for the chick to be hatched."

"Agreed!" stated the materialist. Thus, they placed the egg within the incubator. However, the chick never came out...

The sage, Mr. Alfonso Herrera, author of *Plasmogeny*, managed to create a cell. However, it was a dead cell which never had life.

Hybridization is performed on plants. A branch from one plant is implanted into another, to supposedly improve the fruits. Thus, this is what the know-it-alls do when desiring to improve nature. Nevertheless, what they do is an absurdity, because hybridized plants do not carry the same natural living force of the megalocosm. Thus, the ingested adulterated fruits come to harm the human body. This is from the energetic point of view.

Nonetheless, materialistic scientists feel satisfied with their experiments. They do not want to understand that each tree captures energy. The tree then transforms and retransmits this energy into its fruits. Therefore, when a tree is altered, the energies of the megalocosm are altered also. Thus, the fruit of a hybrid tree is no longer the same because that fruit is the product of an adultery that harms the organisms.

Regardless, materialistic scientists believe that they know when truthfully they indeed do not know. They do not only ignore, but what is worse, they ignore that they ignore.

Artificial inseminations are made with the famous spermatozoon, with the vivifying cells, which are extracted from an organism. Therefore, in this day and age, based on that artificial inception, materialistic scientists think that they are creating life. They do not acknowledge that they are only utilizing what nature has already made.

Let us put on the laboratory table the chemical elements which are needed in order to fabricate a spermatozoon and an ovum. Let us tell the scientists to make the ovum and the spermatozoon. Could they do it? I say that they could. But, would they have life? Could perhaps a living child come out of it? No, a living child can never, ever come out of it because they do not know how to create life.

Therefore, if they are not even capable of creating the seed of a tree, a seed that can germinate, with what proof do they deny the superior or creative intelligences? What is the basis that materialists have in order to deny the creative intelligences? Why do they pronounce themselves against the Eternal One?

Has any materialistic scientist been able to create life? When?

To play with what nature has already made is something easy, but to create life is different. No scientist can do it...

They divide an amoeba into two, they separate its parts on a laboratory table and they unite it with another piece of micro-organism. Subsequently, they exclaim: "Eureka! Eureka! Eureka! We are creating life!" Nonetheless, they are not capable of creating an amoeba.

Therefore, where is the science of these materialistic gentlemen? When have they demonstrated that they can replace Divinity? The reality of facts shows us that they not only ignore, but what is worse, they ignore that they ignore. Facts are what count and until now they cannot demonstrate that they can do it.

They say that the human being comes from the ape. They came out with the theory of the cynocephalus with a tail, the monkey without a tail and the arboreal men, all of them children of the noeptizoids, etc. But, which of these would then be the missing link? On what day have they found a monkey that is capable of speaking, that is gifted with speech? It has not appeared until now. Therefore, these materialistic gentlemen are ludicrous. They only present us suppositions and not facts.

Let us measure the volume of the brain in the best of the apes and let us compare it with the brain of an uncivilized human being that may be found, for instance, in the tribes of Australia. It is obvious that such an ape would not even reach the capacity of speaking.

Therefore are not the materialists refuting the theories of Darwin himself and his henchmen? Does the human being come from the ape? Upon which basis do they sustain this theory? How do they demonstrate it? Until when are we going to wait for the supposed missing link? We want to see that specie of ape speaking like people. That ape has not appeared, therefore such an ape is only a supposition of nonsense that has no reality.

Why do they speak about things that they do not know? Why do they show us so many cheap utopias? It is simply because they have their consciousness asleep, because they have never become interested in carrying out a psychological revolution within themselves and because they lack the practice of Sexual Super-dynamics. Therefore, the crude reality of the facts is that they are hypnotized.

Whosoever does not practice the teachings of the revolution of the dialectic will fall into the same errors as those of the materialistic scientists.

Materialistic scientists continuously come out with many theories. As an example, we will mention that theory of the natural selection of the species. An insignificant mollusk develops, and from it, through the process of selection, other living species emerge. Thus, their selective processes advance until reaching the level of human being. Can they demonstrate this theory? Obviously not!

We do not deny that in each species certain selective processes do exist. For instance, there are birds that migrate at specific times. One is amazed to see them all gathered, how strange they become. Suddenly, they pick up flight in order to cross the ocean and on their way, they die. However, only the strongest ones survive the attempt. The ones that survive the attempt transmit their characteristics to their descendants. This is how the selective law works.

There are species that incessantly struggle against marine monsters and on the basis of so many struggles they become strong. Thus, they transmit their characteristics to their descendants.

There are beasts that on the basis of so many struggles become stronger and stronger each time. Hence, this is how they transmit their psychological characteristics to their descendants.

However, this law of natural selection has never been able to present to us a new species upon the stage of existence. Nonetheless, there are many who have given to this law of natural selection the characteristics of a Creator.

A great deal has also been stated about the protoplasm, that hypothetical protoplasm which was submerged within a salty sea millions of years ago. They allege that from that protoplasm universal life emerged.

The materialistic protists make their henchmen (who are ignorant like themselves) believe that the psychological development of the intellectual animal (mistakenly called a human) comes from the molecular development of the protoplasm and that this psychological development marches parallel to that of the processes of the protoplasm.

The protists demand that the consciousness (or whichever way they may want to call it) must be the outcome of the evolution of the protoplasm throughout the centuries. This is the presumption of the protists, who believe themselves to be gifted with sapience.

Haeckel's atomic monera comes to my memory. The monera is that hypothetical atom that in foregone times was submerged in an aqueous abyss. They state that from this monera all life emerged. This is how Haeckel and his henchmen think.

Never has anything complex (that has not had to undergo different cosmic universal processes) been organized.

The reality is that scientists know nothing about life or death. They do not know where we came from or where we are going. Not by any means do they know what the objective of existence is. Why? It is simply because they have their consciousness asleep, because they have not done the interior revolution of the dialectic, because they are at the level of mass-collective hypnosis due to the lack of the integral revolution that we teach in this book.

Materialistic science marches on the path of error. Materialistic science knows nothing about the origin of the human being. Not by any means does materialistic science know about the inner psychology of the human being.

We do not deny that the law of natural selection has existed. Nevertheless, the law of natural selection has never created anything new.

We do not deny that the species vary throughout time. Nonetheless, the factors of variability of any species only enter into action after their original prototypes have crystallized in the physical world. The original prototypes of any living species previously develop within psychological space, that is, in the superior dimensions of nature.

These original prototypes develop themselves within the superior dimensions which the materialistic scientists deny because they do not perceive them. They do not perceive them because they are psychologically hypnotized.

If they would first come out of their hypnotic state and thereafter talk, then their concepts would be different; nonetheless, they sleep due to the lack of Mental and Sexual Dynamics.

If someone wants to know about the origin of the human being, he has to observe ontogeny. Ontogeny is a recapitulation of phylogeny.

What is ontogeny within anthropology? It is the process of development of the fetus within the maternal womb. If we observe the processes of gestation of a mother, we can

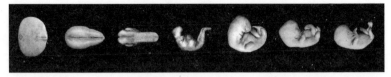

THE ONTOGENY OR DEVELOPMENT OF THE HUMAN FETUS

then evince that ontogeny is a recapitulation of phylogeny. Phylogeny is a state of evolution and transformation that the human race has undergone throughout the centuries.

Thus, these states which the human race has undergone throughout the centuries are recapitulated by the ontogeny within the maternal womb. Therefore, an ontogenic analysis would lead us to the logical conclusion that the human species and other animal species have a resemblance in their origin and come from the psychological space.

However, the law of natural selection with its different variants or factors that produce variation in the human race, only go into action after the species (whichever they might be) have physically crystallized. Before the physical crystallization, evolving psychological processes occur within the living bosom of nature. These evolving psychological processes are unknown to Haeckel and his henchmen, because in fact they know nothing about the origin of the human being.

How is it possible that materialistic scientists state that certain variations exist (whether it is by accident or in a spontaneous manner) in the different types of living species? Is this statement perhaps not a contradiction?

Are not perhaps the materialistic scientists the ones who state that this universe is the result of force, matter and necessity? Then afterwards, they talk to us about spontaneous variants in a universe of force and necessity. How is this possible? This is how they contradict themselves.

A universe of force, matter and necessity does not admit spontaneous or accidental variations. Nonetheless, variations in the species exist due to something which the materialistic scientists themselves do not know. Therefore, materialistic science does not only ignore, but what is worse, it ignores that it ignores.

Psychoanalytical Gnostic anthropology delves profoundly into the past. It sustains that this present human race which nowadays populates the face of the Earth is nothing but a race of intellectual animals mistakenly called human beings (it is up to you whether or not you will become offended by this). However, the truth is that before this race of intellectual animals existed, Lemurian, Hyperborean, and Polar true human beings existed.

The intellectual animals are derived from Atlantis; they were born in Atlantis.

The real humans (during the times of Lemuria in its last days) withdrew from that world scene. These humans left their physical organisms to the superior elemental creatures of the animal kingdoms.

The race of intellectual animals was preceded by the human beings who formerly existed in Lemuria, in the Hyperborean continent and in the northern polar cap (which in that epoch was situated in the equatorial zone). What does psychoanalytic Gnostic anthropology base itself upon in order to affirm this? Why does it state this?

To sustain that this psychoanalytic Gnostic anthropology bases itself not only upon all the traditions that come from the books of ancient Egypt, from the books of the land of the Incas, from the books of the lands of the Mayas, and from Greece, India, Persia, Tibet, etc., but also from the direct investigations of those who have succeeded in awakening their consciousness through a psychological revolution.

Through this book we are delivering all the systems which are necessary in order to awaken the consciousness.

Thus, when you awaken your consciousness, you will be able to investigate and verify for yourselves what I emphatically affirm.

It is necessary to awaken the consciousness in order to touch, see, hear and feel with it and in order to not be a victim of the theories of Haeckel, Darwin, Huxley, and his henchmen.

So, before this race of intellectual animals (derived from Atlantis) existed, three Root Races of human being existed, but how could you verify this when your consciousness is asleep? Therefore, only those who succeed in awakening their consciousness will be able to investigate the Akashic Archives of nature.

How was the First Root Race? In what manner did this race exist? Well, according to the investigations that we have performed, the protoplasmic human beings existed in forgone times around 300 million years ago. At that time even the Earth itself was protoplasmic.

Such a protoplasmic Earth was different. It was not the protoplasm of Haeckel, the salty sea plus thousands of other foolishness that had no confirmation, no!

The protoplasmic Root Race was different. This human Root Race floated in the atmosphere. They still had not fallen upon the humid earth.

How did they reproduce themselves and what was their origin? This race had evolved and devolved within the superior dimensions of nature and the cosmos. Thus, after many evolving processes (which surged forth from its original germ located in the chaos, in the magnus limbus, in the illiaster of the world) they finally crystallized upon an Earth which was also protoplasmic. When that Root Race crystallized, they formed the core, the nucleus, and they could just as well assume gigantic figures as well as reduce themselves to a mathematical point.

Upon what do I base myself in order to affirm this? Upon my awakened consciousness! Have I evinced it? Yes, I have evinced it! If you accept the doctrine of reincarnation, so much the better because I was obviously reincarnated in that Root Race and since I am awakened, I cannot forget the evolving and devolving processes of that race. This is why (acknowledging that you are asleep) I give testimony of it before you, because I must deposit all the data that you need in order for you to awaken.

How did that race multiply? How did they reproduce themselves? Not as Master Blavatsky erroneously stated, that they did it in an asexual manner, that they did not need sex for their reproduction. Such an affirmation is erroneous because the force of the Maha-Chohan, the creative energy of the Third Logos, flows in an overwhelming manner in everything that has been and will be. Their type of reproduction was fissiparous; they sexually expressed themselves in a different way. Their organisms divided themselves the way living cells divide. Biology students know very well how an organic cell divides itself: the cytoplasm with a piece of nucleus becomes separated; they do not ignore this.

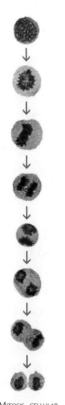

Ever since then, the fissiparous process remained in our blood and continues occurring in our cells by the millions. Is this not true? Who dares to deny it? I present facts! Do you perhaps believe that such cellular processes do not have a root, an origin? If you would think that way it would be an absurdity because there is no cause without an effect and no effect without a cause. Therefore, we have inherited that process. From whom have we inherited it? We have inherited from the human beings of the First Root Race.

The detached organism could continue developing itself thanks to the fact that it continued

MITOSIS, CELLULAR DIVISION

capturing, accumulating protoplasm from the surrounding atmosphere.

Later on in time, the Hyperboreans surged forth. These are the beings of whom Friedrich Nietzsche refers. They were people who lived in the horseshoe shaped lands that surround the North Pole, their septentrional country. Have we evinced this? Yes or no? You have not because your consciousness is asleep. Nonetheless, I have evinced this, because I have my consciousness awakened. So, can I deny it? No, I cannot deny it! Thus, if you consider that I am crazy, well, consider me crazy. Nevertheless, I have to give testimony; I have to always teach the truth no matter what the cost might be.

Thus, the Hyperboreans also existed. However, they were no longer as gelatinous as the protoplasmic human beings. Nonetheless, when I discourse in this manner, I am not referring to the cellular soul of Haeckel within that salty sea nor to the famous atomic monera. Let us leave Haeckel and his henchmen with their absurd theories.

Continuing, I now wish to emphatically state that the Hyperborean Root Race was derived from the protoplasmic Root Race. The Hyperboreans were a more psychic race who reproduced themselves through a kind of budding sexuality. For instance, have you seen the corals on the cliffs of the stormy ocean? How from one coral there sprouts another, and from that one, another, and another? There exist plants which by means of their sprouts they continue multiplying themselves. Thus, the same occurred with the Hyperboreans. Certain sprouts appeared in the father-mother's body. Through these sprouts, this being regulated the sexual force until its sprout was detached and gave rise to a new child. This was the method of reproduction in the Hyperboreans.

In the end, that Root Race submerged itself within the bottom of the stormy Pacific Ocean throughout millions of years of evolutions and devolutions of this fecund nature.

Posteriorly, from the bottom of the seas the gigantic continent Lemuria emerged. The continent Lemuria covered the entire Pacific Ocean. It was here in Lemuria where for the first time the human race rested upon the hard crust of the earth.

So, the Lemurian continent appeared. Nevertheless, the Lemurian continent did not appear through spontaneous generation as Epicurus and his henchmen believed, or through natural selection (a theory that has been elevated to the category of a creative god, which is just a marvelous rhetoric that has come from absurdity).

So, how did it surge forth? In what manner did it?

When in Lemuria the Arboreans or Hyperboreans crystallized, their human bodies took upon a hard shape. Thus, it was in this manner that the Lemurian hermaphrodites appeared. This is how they are symbolized in the gigantic sculptures of Tula, Hidalgo, Mexico. They walked upon the face of the Earth. In the beginning, they reproduced by detaching an egg cell from their organism and this egg cell developed to give origin to a new creature. That was the epoch in which the phallus and the uterus had not yet been formed; that was the

TULA, HIDALGO, MEXICO

epoch in which the lingam and yoni were germinating. That was the epoch in which the ovary had not yet developed.

CALICES OF ORBICELLA ANNULARIS (SYN. MONTASTRAEA ANNULARIS) DANA, MAGNIFIED, SHOWING THE PROCESS OF MULTIPLICATION BY GEMMATION (SMALL CALICLE IN THE MIDDLE), AND BY DIVISION (THE LARGE DOUBLE CALICLE).

The times elapsed in Lemuria and the reproductive system by **gemmation** appeared. Such a system caused astonishment in that epoch. The hermaphrodite's ovary received a fecundating cell, in other words, a spermatozoon, in such a manner that when the egg became detached from the ovary of that hermaphrodite, it was already fecundated.

Upon coming to existence, after a certain time of fecundation, the egg opened up and from there a new child emerged. This is why the Nahuas stated, *"The Children of the Third Sun transformed themselves into birds,"* a wise affirmation from the ancient Nahua culture.

Then, once the end of Lemuria came closer, during their third or fourth sub-race onwards, human beings divided themselves into opposite sexes. Thus, sexual cooperation was then necessary in order to create. Therefore, the present system of sexual cooperation in order to create comes from Lemuria.

It is evident that in order to create, one ovarian egg fecundated by a cell (a spermatozoon) is needed. Thus, only in this manner, in the union of a fertilizing cell with an ovum, is how the original cell with the 48 chromosomes[†] can surge forth, a cell which we indisputably carry within our interior and within which the 48 laws of our creation are represented.

[†] - Modern scientists have not yet discovered two chromosomes related to the vital, ethereal, fourth dimensional aspect.
Thus, they count only 46 physical chromosomes.

Chapter VIII

The Ex-personality and
the Quantum Theory

The cause of the effulgence of the atoms comes from units of energy which are called quanta.

The quanta move themselves within the diamond at half of their usual velocity; their velocity progressively decreases within the air, water, and earth.

An atom is like a vibrometer that produces waves whose momentum flows in accordance with its type.

The emotional attachment of disembodied people diminishes the velocity of the quanta within their ex-personality in such a manner that the radiance from the deceased's ex-personality can become accessible to the retina of a living person. Then, the ex-personality of the deceased person is physically palpable.

The Garcia Peña Case

On a certain day I encountered an old friend of mine on Cinco de Mayo Street in Mexico City. I greeted him raising my arm and I continued on my way. A few days later I met a relative of this friend of mine, who to my surprise told me that Mr. Garcia Peña, my friend whom I had greeted on Cinco de Mayo Street, had died two months ago. Undoubtedly, the ex-personality of this friend of mine made itself tangible because he was emotionally attached to this world in which we live. Thus he was repeating the same actions that he was mechanically accustomed to.

It is indubitable that a close relationship exists between the energetic and atomic personality and the quanta which possess their own vibratory frequency. The disembodied persons customarily unconsciously decrease the quantum vibration of their personalities due to their emotional attachment towards this three-dimensional world. Thus, this is how they make themselves palpable and perceptible.

When the quanta are fast they are not perceived. When they are too slow, they are not perceived either.

Normally, the quanta travel at the speed of light and in a circular way.

The secret of time is hidden within the atom. The concept about time is negative. No one could demonstrate the velocity of time. Time cannot be enclosed in a laboratory.

We place the concept of time between one event and another. The proof of this is in the great number of different calendars.

The attitude that we have at a given instant is what decreases the velocity of the quantum. This same quantum phenomenon is what usually occurs at spiritualistic meetings.

The processes of the cosmos are performed in an eternal now. The rising and setting of the Sun are performed in an eternal instant.

We must move on towards the developing of our own way of thinking. From the energetic point of view, each of us is a mathematical point that allows to serve as a vehicle of specific values, whether they are positive or negative.

Image, values, and identity within the one who annihilated the ego are positive. Death must be considered as a mathematical subtraction.

Reincorporation

Reincorporation is the new principle that explains the incessant incorporation of values within mathematical points.

Energy is indestructible. I do not believe that the quanta can be destroyed. However, it is possible to manage to transform them. Every human being who likes the psychological revolution must reflect upon all that which is related with the quantum phenomena, in order to extract from it the self-concept and the evident self-reflection of the Being.

The study of the quantum can be performed by that one who through his actions can live the Mental Dynamics in his own flesh and that through it achieves the emancipation of his mind.

Super-discipline

The super-discipline and perfection of the physical body are achieved by means of naturopathic medicine.

When a super-discipline exists, it is obvious that we will be able to obtain direct wisdom from the archaeological documents.

By having super-discipline we will comprehend and accept that we have to take life, willingly, as a gymnasium.

Whosoever submits himself to super-discipline can expect great triumphs.

Those who live by super-discipline will have to be strong in order to bear the "solitude of the path."

Evident Self-reflection

In order to comprehend evident self-reflection, one needs to study the *Epistle* of James which is written for those who work in the Great Work, in the revolution of the dialectic.

It is necessary that the Great Work and the psychological work become supported by faith, because faith is manifested through deeds.

Whosoever knows how to handle his tongue will dominate his body and will dominate others; thus, as a consequence he will march in an ascending manner in the Great Work and in the psychological work.

As we advance in the practice of these psychological teachings, we must avoid falling into another psychological error

DHARMPALA IS SANSKRIT FOR "PROTECTOR OF DHARMA." THIS PAINTING DEPICTS THE
DHARMAPALA MAHAKALA (WHICH MEANS "GREAT TIME"), WHOSE HINDU EQUIVILIENT IS SHIVA.
MAHAKALA IS THE FORCE THAT SUSTAINS THE UNIVERSE WITH HIS CONSORT, KALI.

which is that of becoming boastful. We must also not become conceited in order to triumph in the Great Work and in the evident self-reflection.

Every alchemist, Kabbalist, and psychologist must have faith. Faith is not empirical; we have to fabricate it. Faith is fabricated by studying oneself and by experimenting with oneself.

The Mystery

The Dharmapalas are the tremendous Lords of Power who have launched themselves against the materialistic aberrations of the Chinese communists.

I will personally be in Tibet because great things are gestated in this sacred place. I will be helping the Tibetans to put an end to the traces of abominations that the Chinese have left.

Shangri-la is located within the fourth dimension and it is a city in the Jinn State. The Venerable Master Kout-Humi is found there.

Tibet is very similar to Egypt; the monks do not ignore the works of mummification. In the past, the Tibetan monks carried their mummies to the volcanic craters where the monasteries are found.

I do not have any type of fear in order to affirm that I am a Tibetan lama. You may ask yourselves how is it that I am here and there. Well, this is possible by means of the power of ubiquity.

Yes, momentarily I am here in Mexico, and at the same time in Tibet, in the valley of Adi-tattva. In this valley, sacred processions are performed. The monastery is located on the right side of the valley. Before, the monastery was located in the third dimension. Now, it is submerged within the fourth vertical. In its interior, the building has large halls where objective works are performed. As a lama, I have a small work room. The Dharmapalas meet on the patio of the monastery.

The order is formed by 201 members. The superior rank is constituted by 72 Brahmans. This order is the one that governs the destinies of humanity.

Tibet has always been invaded by the English and Chinese, but they have always had to leave due to the tremendous power of the Dharmapalas.

The Avatar

Avatars cannot forget the social matter; this is why Quetzalcoatl manifested himself in two aspects: the social and the psychological.

In my case I have been concerned with these two aspects: human problems (intended to be solved by means of the revolution of the consciousness in a dialectic manner) and the problems of capital and labor (intended to be solved by means of POSCLA).

EXPERIENCE:

"They gave him a flagstaff which represented problems; they made him enter into a secret sanctuary and he found the Patriarch St. Augustine in that sanctuary. The Patriarch took a voluminous book from the bookcase and told him: 'I will teach you a mantra in order to make the fire blaze.' He opened the book... He lit the coals in the brazier... He pronounced the mantra "M" and the fire became inflamed. When he came out, he learned to sing the mantra in order to stir up the flame.

"St. Augustine, the Patriarch dressed with his priestly robes, returned towards the front of the altar of the temple and the Master Samael also... They placed a frying pan in his right hand... as if to say: 'You have everything you need in the palm of your hand.'

"Together, they performed a great chain...

"'We will accompany you by forming this great battle.'"

"Thus, in this manner, the White Brotherhood accompanies him..."

Disgracefully, the younger Gnostic brethren have not studied; they have not lived my doctrine which I have delivered throughout so many years in order for them to attain the psychological liberation. Thus, they themselves have wanted to sabotage the Great Work of the White Brotherhood...

We have delivered the keys of revolutionary psychology and of POSCLA. However, through them, we do not want to climb to positions; we do not want to live on the national budget either. The only thing that we want is to be useful to humanity, to serve by giving psychological norms which I myself have experienced so that the intellectual animal can achieve integral revolution...

The mission of an Avatar is not only related with religious matters but it also includes the political and psychological matters of nations.

"We need to change within ourselves; we
need to alter within our own individuality
the abominable factors which produce
misery and pain in the world."

Chapter IX
The Individual and Society

Society is the extension of the individual. If the individual is covetous, cruel, pitiless, egotistical, etc., then the society will be likewise. It is necessary to be sincere with oneself. Each one of us is a degenerate; therefore, our society inevitably has to be degenerated. This cannot be resolved by the terrible monster of materialism. This can only be resolved by the individual on the basis of his integral revolution.

The hour to reflect on our own destiny has arrived. Violence does not resolve anything. Violence can only lead us to failure. We need peace, serenity, reflection, comprehension.

The problem of the world is the problem of the individual. Bloody revolutions do not resolve anything. The problem of having the consciousness bottled up can only be resolved by means of intelligence.

Only by means of intelligence is it possible for us to convert the intellectual animal first into a Man and afterwards into a Superman. Only by means of the revolution of the dialectic is it possible for us to overcome the terrible monster of materialism.

The human society is the extension of the individual. Therefore, if we really want a radical change, if we want a better world, we need to then change individually. We need to change within ourselves; we need to alter within our own individuality the abominable factors which produce misery and pain in the world. Let us remember that the human-mass is the sum of the individuals. If each individual changes, then the human-mass will inevitably change.

It is urgent to terminate egotism and cultivate Christ-centrism. Thus, only in this manner can we make a better world. It is indispensable to eliminate the covetousness and the cruelty that each one of us carries within. Thus, only in this manner, by each individual changing, is how society will change, because society is just the extension of the individual.

Pain, hunger and confusion exist. However, none of this can be eliminated through the absurd procedures of violence. Those who want to transform the world based on bloody revolutions and drugs, or with coups-d'etats and executions by shootings are totally mistaken because violence engenders more violence and hatred engenders more hatred. We need peace if what we want is to resolve the problems of humanity.

Darkness is not dissolved with blows or with atheism, but rather by bringing about the light. Neither is error dissolved by fighting it face to face, but rather by disseminating the truth without having to attack the error. How ever far the truth advances, in that same measure error will have to retreat. One does not have to resist what is negative, but instead one has to unconditionally practice the positive and teach its advantages by practicing. By attacking the error, we will provoke the hatred of those who err.

What we need is to disseminate the light of the revolution of the dialectic in order to dissipate the darkness.

It is urgent to analyze the fundamental principles of Marxist dialectics in order to demonstrate to the world the tremendous reality that indeed the principles from Marxist dialectics do not resist an in-depth analysis and are absolutely nothing but cheap sophistry.

If we want to overcome the darkness let us make Light. Let us not spill blood. The hour of being comprehensive has arrived.

It is necessary to study our own "I" if we really love our fellowmen. It is indispensable to comprehend that only by putting an end to the factors of egotism and cruelty (that each one of us carries within) can we create a better world, a world without hunger and fear.

Society is the individual. The world is the individual. Therefore, if the individual fundamentally changes, the world will inevitably change.

The consciousness is in critical danger and only by radically transforming ourselves as individuals can we save ourselves and save humanity.

To the Consciousness

Sleeping consciousness...

How different thou would be if thou would awaken...

Thou would know the seven paths of happiness,

The light of thy love would shine everywhere,

The birds would rejoice within the mystery of thy forests,

The light of the spirit would gleam, and happily in chorus the elementals would sing verses for thee.

Enlightenment

In an orderly way you must practice the teachings of the revolution of the dialectic. From this very moment initiate your integral revolution. You must dedicate time to your psychological-self, because the way you are, as alive as you are, with that tremendous "I" within, you are a failure.

I want you to resolve to radically die in all the levels of your mind.

Many are those who complain that they cannot travel in the Astral World at will. Astral travel ceases to be a problem when one awakens the consciousness. The sleepy ones are good for nothing.

I have delivered the science that is necessary in order to achieve the awakening of consciousness within this book, *The Revolution of the Dialectic*. Do not commit the error of reading this book like someone who reads a newspaper. Profoundly study this book for many years; live it, practice it.

I advise patience and serenity for those who complain of not having achieved enlightenment. Enlightenment comes to us when we dissolve the pluralized "I"; when we have indeed died within the 49 levels of the subconsciousness.

Those who go around coveting occult powers, those who utilize Sex Yoga as a pretext in order to seduce women, are totally mistaken. Such people march in the opposite direction, opposite to the goals and disciplines that Universal Gnosticism establishes.

You must work on the Three Factors of the revolution of consciousness in an orderly and perfect manner.

Do not commit the error of committing adultery and fornicating. Abandon the habit of being like a butterfly, that is, those who like to flutter about from one flower to the next, from one school to another school. Indeed, those who act like that are candidates for the abyss and the Second Death.

Abandon self-justification and self-consideration. Become enemies of yourselves if indeed what you really want is to radically die. Thus, only in this manner will you achieve enlightenment.

Start from scratch, from point zero. Abandon mystical pride, mythomania, the tendency to consider yourselves super-transcended, because all of you are merely intellectual animals condemned to the pain of living.

It becomes urgent and unpostponable to make an inventory of yourselves in order for you to know what you really are.

Be humble in order to attain enlightenment. Thus, after attaining it, be more humble still.

Glossary

Antichrist: The force or energy which is polarized in the opposite vibration of the energy or force of the Christ. The Christ is the force of light which gives rise to all life: it is creative, illuminating, and marked by pure, selfless love or compassion. The energy or force of the Antichrist is destructive, bringing darkness, selfishness, and hatred. According to Universal Gnosticism, the intellect of each human being is the Antichrist, because the intellect of the contemporary human being is selfish, filled with darkness and hatred, and seeks to create destruction through the inventions, books, movies, words, and concepts it produces. Definitely, the Antichrist is not a particular person, but all people. Obviously, the Antichrist itself exists deep within each person and expresses itself in many ways.

Army of the Word: A reference to Elohim Sabbaoth (Hebrew), the army or host of gods and goddesses.

Astral: This term is dervied from "pertaining to or proceeding from the stars," but in the esoteric knowledge it refers to the emotional aspect of the fifth dimension, which in Hebrew is called Hod.

Astral Body: What is commonly called the Astral Body is not the true Astral Body, it is rather the Lunar Protoplasmatic Body, also known as the Kama Rupa (Sanskrit, "body of desires") or "dream body" (Tibetan rmi-lam-gyi lus). The true Astral Body is Solar (being superior to Lunar Nature) and must be created, as the Master Jesus indicated in the Gospel of John 3:5-6, "Except a man be born of water and of the Spirit, he cannot enter into the kingdom of God. That which is born of the flesh is flesh; and that which is born of the Spirit is spirit." The Solar Astral Body is created as a result of the Third Initiation of Major Mysteries (Serpents of Fire), and is perfected in the Third Serpent of Light. In Tibetan Buddhism, the Solar Astral Body is known as the illusory body (sgyu-lus). This body is related to the emotional center and to the sephirah Hod.

"Really, only those who have worked with the Maithuna (White Tantra) for many years can possess the Astral Body." - Samael Aun Weor, *The Elimination of Satan's Tail*

Avatar: From the Sanskrit avatarah, meaning descent (of a deity from heaven), avatar: ava, down + tarati, he crosses. An incarnation of the cosmic, universal Christ (Vishnu, Chokmah). Samael Aun Weor used the term "avatar" to mean "messenger."

"The reincarnated Christ expresses himself through every authentic Avatar. " - Samael Aun Weor, *The Pistis Sophia Unveiled*

"...the Omni-merciful, the infinitude that sustains all, the very, very sacred Absolute Sun, periodically sends Avatars, Saviors, to this valley of tears. These sacred individuals, these messengers, these Saviors, are living incarnations of the Omni-merciful. Nevertheless, this lunar race, this perverse race of Adam, mortally hates such helpers. [...] The blessed Krishna, the blessed Buddha, the blessed Lama, the blessed Mohammed, the loving, essential Ashiata Shiemash, Moses, Quetzalcoatl (and many others) were all Avatars. The doctrine of all Avatars has its roots in the three basic factors of the revolution of the consciousness: to be born, to die, and to sacrifice the self for humanity." - Samael Aun Weor, *The Doomed Aryan Race*

Avitchi: (Sanskrit) "Hell."

Bodhisattva: (Sanskrit) Literally, the Sanskrit term Bodhi means enlightenment or wisdom, while Sattva means essence or goodness; therefore, the term Bodhisattva literally means "essence of wisdom." The Tibetan translation of this word is jangchub sempa. Jangchub (Sanskrit bodhi) means enlightenment, and sempa (Sanskrit sattva) means hero or a being, therefore meaning "enlightened hero." The word jangchub is from jang, "the overcoming and elimination of all obstructive forces," and chub, "realization of full knowledge." Sempa is a reference to great compassion. The 14th Dalai Lama said, "...bodhisattvas are beings who, out of intense compassion, never shift their attention away from sentient beings; they are purpetually concerned for the welfare of all beings, and they dedicate themselves entirely to securing that welfare. Thus the very name bodhisattva indicates a being who, through wisdom, heroically focuses on the attainment of enlightenment out of compassionate concern for all beings. The word itself conveys the key qualities of such an infinitely altruistic being."

"We, the bodhisattvas of compassion who love humanity immensely, state: as long as there is a single tear in any human eye, as long as there is even one suffering heart, we refuse to accept the happiness of Nirvana... We must seek the means to become more and more useful to this wretched, suffering humanity." - Samael Aun Weor, *The Major Mysteries*

In the esoteric or secret teachings of Tibet and Gnosticism, a Bodhisattva is a human being who has reached the Fifth Initiation of Fire (Tiphereth) and has chosen to continue working by means of the Straight Path, renouncing the easier Spiral Path (in Nirvana), and returning instead to help suffering humanity. By means of this sacrifice, this individual incarnates the Christ (Avalokitesvara), thereby embodying the supreme source of wisdom and compassion. This is the entrance to the Direct Path to complete liberation from the ego, a route that only very few take, due to the fact that one must pay the entirety of one's karma in one life. Those who have taken this road have been the most remarkable figures in human history: Jesus, Buddha, Mohamed, Krishna, Moses, Padmasambhava, Milarepa, Joan of Arc, Fu-Xi, and many others whose names are not remembered or known. Of course, even among bodhisattvas there are many levels of Being: to be a bodhisattva does not mean that one is enlightened. Interestingly, the Christ in Hebrew is called Chokmah, which means "wisdom," and in Sanskrit the same is Vishnu, the root of the word "wisdom." It is Vishnu who sent his Avatars into the world in order to guide humanity. These avatars were Krishna, Buddha, Rama, and the Avatar of this age: the Avatar Kalki.

"The truly humble Bodhisattva never praises himself. The humble Bodhisattva says, 'I am just a miserable slug from the mud of the earth, I am a nobody. My person has no value. The work is what is worthy.' The Bodhisattva is the human soul of a Master. The Master is the internal God." - Samael Aun Weor, *The Aquarian Message*

"Let it be understood that a Bodhisattva is a seed, a germ, with the possibility of transcendental, divine development by means of pressure coming from the Height." - Samael Aun Weor, *The Pistis Sophia Unveiled*

Cathexis: 1. Concentration of emotional energy on an object or idea. 2. (from Freudian Psychoanalysis) the libidinal energy invested in some idea or person or object; "Freud thought of cathexis as a psychic analog of an electrical charge." In Universal Gnosticism, cathexis has varying types: Bound Cathexis is the psychic energy that is under the control of the Inner Being. Loose Cathexis is the energy utilized by the ego. Free Cathexis is the energy developed by the physical body; this energy is normally absorbed by the ego and in turn develops and feeds more ego. The Revolution requires that the free cathexis and the loose cathexis, or in other words, all the energies of the psyche and body, be absorbed by the Inner Being. This requires the complete removal of all ego.

Causa causorum: (Latin) "Cause of Causes."

Centers, Seven: The human being has seven centers of psychological activity. The first five are the Intellectual, Emotional, Motor, Instinctive, and Sexual Centers. However, through inner development one learns how to utilize the Superior Emotional and Superior Intellectual Centers. Most people do not use these two at all.

Christ: Derived from the Greek Christos, "the Anointed One," and Krestos, whose esoteric meaning is "fire." The word Christ is a title, not a personal name.

"Christ is not an individual. The Cosmic Christ is impersonal, universal, and is beyond individuality, personality, beyond the "I." Yet, Christ is a cosmic force that can express Himself through any human being who is properly prepared. [...] Among the Chinese, Christ is Fu Ji. Among the Mexicans, Christ is Quetzalcoatl, who was the Messiah and the transformer of the Toltecs. Among the Japanese, Christ is Amida, who has the power of opening doors of Gokurak (paradise). Within the Zoroastrian cult, Christ is Ahura-Mazda. The Germanic Eddas cite the Kristos, who is the God of their theogony, similar to Jesus of Nazareth, who was born on the day of Nativity, the 25th of December at midnight, the same as the Nordic Christs Odin, Wotan, and Belen. The Gospel of Krishna, within millenary India, is similar to the Christian Gospel. In the ancient Egypt of the Pharaohs, Christ was Osiris, and whosoever incarnated him was an Osirified one. Hermes Trismegistus is the Egyptian Christ; He incarnated Osiris. Every human being that achieves the assimilation of the Christ substance is converted into a living Christ. [...] Indeed, Christ is a Sephirothic Crown (Kether, Chokmah and Binah) of incommensurable wisdom, whose purest atoms shine within Chokmah, the world of the Ophanim. Christ is not the Monad, Christ is not the Theosophical Septenary; Christ is not the Jivan-Atman. Christ is the Central Sun. Christ is the ray that unites us to the Absolute." - Samael Aun Weor, *The Initiatic Path in the Arcana of Tarot and Kabbalah*

"The Gnostic Church adores the Savior of the World, Jesus. The Gnostic Church knows that Jesus incarnated Christ, and that is why they adore him. Christ is not a human nor a divine individual. Christ is a title given to all fully self-realised Masters. Christ is the Army of the Voice. Christ is the Verb. The Verb is far beyond the body, the soul and the Spirit. Everyone who is able to incarnate the Verb receives in fact the title of Christ. Christ is the Verb itself. It is necessary for everyone of us to incarnate the Verb (Word). When the Verb becomes flesh in us we speak with the verb of light. In actuality, several Masters have incarnated the Christ. In secret India, the Christ Yogi Babaji has lived for millions of years; Babaji is immortal. The Great Master of Wisdom Kout Humi also incarnated the Christ. Sanat Kumara, the founder of the Great College of Initiates of the White Lodge, is another living Christ. In the past, many incarnated the Christ. In the present, some have incarnated the Christ. In the future many will incarnate the Christ. John the Baptist also incarnated the Christ. John the Baptist is a living Christ. The difference between Jesus and the other Masters that also incarnated the Christ has to do with Hierarchy. Jesus is the highest Solar Initiate of the Cosmos..." - Samael Aun Weor, *The Perfect Matrimony*

City of Nine Gates: A reference to the human body which has nine openings or "gates."

Consciousness: "Wherever there is life, there exists the consciousness. Consciousness is inherent to life as humidity is inherent to water." - Samael Aun Weor, *Fundamental Notions of Endocrinology and Criminology*

From various dictionaries: 1. The state of being conscious; knowledge of one's own existence, condition, sensations, mental operations, acts, etc. 2. Immediate knowledge or perception of the presence of any object, state, or sensation. 3. An alert cognitive state in which you are aware of yourself and your situation. In Universal Gnosticism, the range of potential consciousness is allegorized in the Ladder of Jacob, upon which the angels ascend and descend. Thus there are higher and lower levels of consciousness, from the level of demons at the bottom, to highly realized angels in the heights.

"It is vital to understand and develop the conviction that consciousness has the potential to increase to an infinite degree." - The 14th Dalai Lama.

"Light and consciousness are two phenomena of the same thing; to a lesser degree of consciousness, corresponds a lesser degree of light; to a greater degree of consciousness, a greater degree of light." - Samael Aun Weor, *The Esoteric Treatise of Hermetic Astrology*

Darwin, Charles Robert: (1809–1882) An English naturalist, grandson of Erasmus Darwin. He firmly established the theory of organic evolution known as Darwinism. He studied medicine at Edinburgh and for the ministry at Cambridge but lost interest in both professions during the training. His interest in natural history led to his friendship with the botanist J. S. Henslow; through him came the opportunity to make a five-year cruise (1831–36) as official naturalist aboard the Beagle. This started Darwin on a career of accumulating and assimilating data that resulted in the formulation of his concept of evolution. He spent the remainder of his life carefully and methodically working over the information from his copious notes and from every other available source. Independently, A. R. Wallace had worked out a theory similar to Darwin's. Both men first published summaries of their ideas simultaneously in 1858. In 1859, Darwin set forth the structure of his theory and massive support for it in the Origin of Species, supplemented and elaborated in his many later books, notably The Descent of Man (1871). Darwin also formulated a theory of the origin of coral reefs.

Darwinism: A concept of evolution developed in the mid-19th cent. by Charles Robert Darwin. Darwin's meticulously documented observations led him to question the then current belief in special creation of each species. After years of studying and correlating the voluminous notes he had made as naturalist on H.M.S. Beagle, he was prompted by the submission (1858) of an almost identical theory by A. R. Wallace to present his evidence for the descent of all life from a common ancestral origin; his Origin of Species was published in 1859. Darwin observed (as had Malthus) that although all organisms tend to reproduce in a geometrically increasing ratio, the numbers of a given species remain more or less constant. From this he deduced that there is a continuing struggle for existence, for survival. He pointed out the existence of variations—differences among members of the same species—and suggested that the variations that prove helpful to a plant or an animal in its struggle for existence better enable it to survive and reproduce. These favorable variations are thus transmitted to the offspring of the survivors and spread to the entire species over successive generations. This process he called the principle of Natural Selection (the expression "survival of the fittest" was later coined by Herbert Spencer). In the same way, sexual selection (factors influencing the choice of mates among animals) also plays a part. In developing his theory that the origin and diversification of species results from gradual accumulation of individual modifications, Darwin was greatly influenced by Sir Charles Lyell's treatment of the doctrine of uniformitarianism. Darwin's evidence for evolution rested on the data of comparative anatomy, especially the study of homologous structures in different species and of rudimentary (vestigial) organs; of the recapitulation of past racial history in individual embryonic development (phylogeny); of geographical distribution, extensively documented by Wallace; of the immense variety in forms of plants and animals (to the degree that often one species is not distinct from another); and, to a lesser degree, of paleontology. As originally formulated, Darwinism did not distinguish between acquired characteristics, which are not transmissible by heredity, and genetic variations, which are inheritable. Modern knowledge of heredity—especially the concept of mutation, which provides an explanation of how variations may arise—has supplemented and modified the theory, but in its basic outline Darwinism has been universally accepted by scientists for the last century. However, increasing evidence is calling the theory into question, in spite of the vigorous resistence of the scientific community, who does not want to let go of this cherished theory.

Devolution: (Latin) From devolvere: backwards evolution, degeneration. The natural mechanical inclination for all matter and energy in nature to return towards their state of inert uniformity. Related to the Arcanum Ten: Retribution, the Wheel of Samsara. Devolution is the inverse process of evolution. As evolution is the complication of matter or energy, devolution is the slow process of nature to simplify matter or energy by applying forces to it. Through devolution, protoplasmic matter and energy descend, degrade, and increase in density within the infradimensions of nature to finally reach the center of the earth where they attain their ultimate state of inert uniformity. Devolution transfers the psyche, moral values, consciousness, or psychological responsibilities to inferior degradable organisms (Klipoth) through the surrendering of our psychological values to animal behaviors, especially sexual degeneration.

Divine Mother: "Among the Aztecs, she was known as Tonantzin, among the Greeks as chaste Diana. In Egypt she was Isis, the Divine Mother, whose veil no mortal has lifted. There is no doubt at all that esoteric Christianity has never forsaken the worship of the Divine Mother Kundalini. Obviously she is Marah, or better said, RAM-IO, MARY. What orthodox religions did not specify, at least with regard to the exoteric or public circle, is the aspect of Isis in her individual human form. Clearly, it was taught only in secret to the Initiates that this Divine Mother exists individually within each human being. It cannot be emphasized enough that Mother-God, Rhea, Cybele, Adonia, or whatever we wish to call her, is a variant of our own individual Being in the here and now. Stated explicitly, each of us has our own particular, individual Divine Mother." - Samael Aun Weor, *The Great Rebellion*

Drukpa: (Also known variously as Druk-pa, Dugpa, Brugpa, Dag dugpa or Dad dugpa) The term Drukpa comes from from Dzongkha and Tibetan 'brug yul, which means "country of Bhutan," and is composed of Druk, "dragon," and pa, "person." In Asia, the word refers to the people of Bhutan, a country between India and Tibet.

Drukpa can also refer to a large sect of Buddhism which broke from the Kagyug-pa "the Ones of the Oral Tradition." They considered themselves as the heirs of the indian Gurus: their teaching, which goes back to Vajradhara, was conveyed through Dakini, from Naropa to Marpa and then to the ascetic and mystic poet Milarepa. Later on, Milarepa's disciples founded new monasteries, and new threads appeared, among which are the Karmapa and the Drukpa. All those schools form the Kagyug-pa order, in spite of episodic internal quarrels and extreme differences in practice. The Drukpa sect is recognized by their ceremonial large red hats, but it should be known that they are not the only "Red Hat" group (the Nyingmas, founded by Padmasambhava, also use red hats). The Drukpas have established a particular worship of the Dorje (Vajra, or thunderbolt, a symbol of the phallus).

Samael Aun Weor wrote repeatedly in many books that the "Drukpas" practice and teach Black Tantra, by means of the expelling of the sexual energy. If we analyze the word, it is clear that he is referring to "Black Dragons," or people who practice Black Tantra. He was not referring to all the people of Bhutan, or all members of the Buddhist Drukpa sect. Such a broad condemnation would be as ridiculous as the one made by those who condemn all Jews for the crucifixion of Jesus.

"In 1387, with just reason, the Tibetan reformer Tsong Khapa cast every book of Necromancy that he found into flames. As a result, some discontent Lamas formed an alliance with the aboriginal Bhons, and today they form a powerful sect of black magic in the regions of Sikkim, Bhutan, and Nepal, submitting themselves to the most abominable black rites." - Samael Aun Weor, *The Revolution of Beelzebub*

Ego: The multiplicity of contradictory psychological elements that we have inside are in their sum the "ego." Each one is also called "an ego" or an "I." Every ego is a psychological defect which produces suffering. The ego is three (related to our three brains or three centers of psychological processing), seven (capital sins), and legion (in their infinite variations).

"The ego is the root of ignorance and pain." - Samael Aun Weor, *The Esoteric Treatise of Hermetic Astrology*

"The Being and the ego are incompatible. The Being and the ego are like water and oil. They can never be mixed... The annihilation of the psychic aggregates (egos) can be made possible only by radically comprehending our errors through meditation and by the evident Self-reflection of the Being." - Samael Aun Weor, *The Pistis Sophia Unveiled*

Elohim: (Hebrew) From אלהים, or the letters aleph, lamed, he, yod, and mem. It carries many meanings. Fundamental are its components: El means "God," Eloah means "Goddess," so Elohim can be read both as a plural word for "Gods and Goddesses" and as a descriptive term for a single androgynous being. The term is commonly used as a reference to the Cosmocreator Archangels, the "seven spirits before the Throne."

Evolution: "Evolution is a process of complication of energy." - Samael Aun Weor, *The Perfect Matrimony*

"It is not possible for the true Human Being (the Self-realized Being) to appear through the mechanics of evolution. We know very well that evolution and its twin sister devolution are nothing else but two laws which constitute the mechanical axis of all Nature. One evolves to a certain perfectly defined point, and then the devolving process follows. Every ascent is followed by a descent and vice-versa." - Samael Aun Weor, *Revolutionary Psychology*.

Gemmation: The formation of a new individual, either animal or vegetable, by a process of budding; an asexual method of reproduction; gemmulation; gemmiparity.

Gnosis: (Greek) Knowledge.

1. The word Gnosis refers to the knowledge we acquire through our own experience, as opposed to knowledge that we are told or believe in. Gnosis - by whatever name in history or culture - is conscious, experiential knowledge, not merely intellectual or conceptual knowledge, belief, or theory. This term is synonymous with the Hebrew "daath" and the Sanskrit "jna."

2. The tradition that embodies the core wisdom or knowledge of humanity.

"Gnosis is the flame from which all religions sprouted, because in its depth Gnosis is religion. The word "religion" comes from the Latin word "religare," which implies "to link the Soul to God"; so Gnosis is the very pure flame from where all religions sprout, because Gnosis is Knowledge, Gnosis is Wisdom." - Samael Aun Weor, *The Esoteric Path*

"The secret science of the Sufis and of the Whirling Dervishes is within Gnosis. The secret doctrine of Buddhism and of Taoism is within Gnosis. The sacred magic of the Nordics is within Gnosis. The wisdom of Hermes, Buddha, Confucius, Mohammed and Quetzalcoatl, etc., etc., is within Gnosis. Gnosis is the Doctrine of Christ." - Samael Aun Weor, *The Revolution of Beelzebub*

Hanasmuss: "The Twice Born who does not reduce his Lunar Ego to cosmic dust converts himself into an abortion of the Cosmic Mother. He becomes a Marut, and there exist thousands of types of Maruts. Certain oriental sects and some Muslim tribes commit the lamentable error of rendering cult to all of those families of Maruts. Every Marut, every Hanasmuss (plural: Hanasmussen) has in fact two personalities: one White and another Black (one Solar and another Lunar). The Innermost, the Being dressed with the Solar Electronic Bodies, is the White Personality of the Hanasmuss, and the pluralized "I" dressed with the Protoplasmic Lunar Bodies is the Hanasmuss' Black Personality. Therefore, these Maruts have a double center of gravity." In synthesis, everyone who has ego is a Hanasmuss. For more information, see the lecture entitled "The Master Key," available at gnosticteachings.org.

Haeckel, Ernst Heinrich: (1834–1919) A German biologist and philosopher. Ernst Haeckel, much like Herbert Spencer, was always quotable, even when wrong. Although best known for the famous statement "ontogeny recapitulates phylogeny," he also coined many words commonly used by biologists today, such as phylum, phylogeny, and ecology. On the other hand, Haeckel also stated that "politics is applied biology," a quote used by Nazi propagandists. The Nazi party, rather unfortunately, used not only Haeckel's quotes, but also Haeckel's justifications for racism, nationalism and social darwinism. Although trained as a physician, Haeckel abandoned his practice in 1859 after reading Darwin's *Origin of Species*. Always suspicious of teleological and mystical explanation, Haeckel used the Origin as ammunition both to attack entrenched religious dogma and to build his own unique world view.

Hermaphrodite: A Hermaphrodite is a Human Being who physically produces sperms and ovums within their own masculine and feminine sexual genitalia. In order to create they fecundate themselves; they physically unite the outcome of their own two sexual polarities (sperm and ovum) by means of willpower.

Homo Nosce Te Ipsum: Latin for the Greek phrase gnothi seauton: "Know thyself," a precept inscribed in gold letters over the portico of the temple at Delphi.

Human Being: According to Gnostic anthropology, a true Human Being is an individual who has conquered the animal nature within and has thus created the Soul, the Mercabah of the Kabbalists, the Sahu of the Egyptians, the To Soma Heliakon of the Greeks: this is "the Body of Gold of the Solar Man." A true Human Being is one with the Monad, the Inner Spirit. A true Human Being has reconquered the innocence and perfection of Eden, and has become what Adam was intended to be: a King of Nature, having power of Nature. The Intellectual Animal, however, is controlled by nature, and thus is not a true Human Being. Examples of true Human Beings are all those great saints of all ages and cultures: Jesus, Moses, Mohammed, Krishna, and many others whose names were never known by the public.

Hydrogen: (From *hydro-* water, *gen-* generate, genes, genesis, etc.) The hydrogen is the simplest element on the periodic table and in Gnosticism it is recognized as the element that is the building block of all forms of matter. Hydrogen is a packet of solar light. The solar light (the light that comes from the sun) is the reflection of the Okidanok, the Cosmic Christ, which creates and sustains every world. This element is the fecundated water, generated water (hydro). The water is the source of all life. Everything that we eat, breathe and all of the impressions that we receive are in the form of various structures of hydrogen. Samael Aun Weor often will place a note (Do, Re, Mi...) and a number related with the vibration and atomic weight (level of complexity) with a particular hydrogen. For example, Samael Aun Weor constantly refers to the Hydrogen Si-12. "Si" is the highest note in the octave and it is the result of the notes that come before it. This particular hydrogen is always related to the forces of Yesod, which is the synthesis and coagulation of all food, air and impressions that we have previously received. Food begins at Do-768, air begins at Do-384, and impressions begin at Do-48.

Hyperboreans: A nation mentioned in Greek mythology. The name means "beyond the North Wind," thus they are supposed to have been somewhere north of Greece, but the name also means "beyond the mountains" and "those who carry (merchandise) across." Apollo was said to spend the winter months among them, and his mother Leto was presumed to have been born in their land. Perseus went there searching for the Gorgon, and Heracles chased the Cerynitian hind to their country. The writer Pindar represented them as a blessed people untouched by human afflictions. H. P. Blavatsky places their country around the North Pole, saying it was "The Land of the Eternal Sun," beyond Boreas, the God of Winter. She asserts that this land was of a near tropical climate.

Illiaster: The primordial seed of creation.

Intellectual Animal: When the Intelligent Principle, the Monad, sends its spark of consciousness into Nature, that spark enters into manifestation as a simple mineral. Gradually, over millions of years, that spark gathers experience and evolves up the chain of life until it perfects itself in the level of the mineral kingdom. It then graduates into the plant kingdom, and subsequently into the animal kingdom. With each ascension the spark receives new capacities and higher grades of complexity. In the animal kingdom it learns procreation by ejaculation. When that animal intelligence enters into the human kingdom, it receives a new capacity: reasoning, the intellect; it is now an animal with intellect: an Intellectual Animal. That spark must then perfect itself in the human kingdom in order to become a complete and perfect Human Being, an entity that has conquered and transcended everything that belongs to the lower kingdoms. Unfortunately, very few Intellectual Animals perfect themselves; most remain enslaved by their animal nature, and thus are reabsorbed by Nature, a process belonging to the devolving side of life and called by all the great religions Hell or the Second Death.

Internal Worlds: The many dimensions beyond the physical world. These dimensions are both subjective and objective. To know the objective internal worlds (the Astral Plane, or Nirvana, or the Klipoth) one must first know one's own personal, subjective internal worlds, because the two are intimately associated.

"Whosoever truly wants to know the internal worlds of the planet Earth or of the solar system or of the galaxy in which we live, must previously know his intimate world, his individual, internal life, his own internal worlds. Man, know thyself, and thou wilt know the Universe and its Gods. The more we explore this internal world called "myself," the more we will comprehend that we simultaneously live in two worlds, in two realities, in two confines: the external and the internal. In the same way that it is indispensable for one to learn how to walk in the external world so as not to fall down into a precipice, or not get lost in the streets of the city, or to select one's friends, or not associate with the perverse ones, or not eat poison, etc.; likewise, through the psychological work upon oneself we learn how to walk in the internal world, which is explorable only through Self-observation." - Samael Aun Weor, *Revolutionary Psychology*

Through the work in Self-observation, we develop the capacity to awaken where previously we were asleep: including in the objective internal worlds.

Kabbalah: (Hebrew קבלה) Alternatively spelled Cabala, Qabalah from the Hebrew קבלה KBLH or QBL, "to receive." An ancient esoteric teaching hidden from the uninitiated, whose branches and many forms have reached throughout the world. The true Kabbalah is the science and language of the Superior Worlds and is thus objective, complete and without flaw; it is said that "All enlightened beings agree," and their natural agreement is a function of the awakened consciousness. The Kabbalah is the language of that consciousness, thus disagreement regarding its meaning and interpretation is always due to the subjective elements in the psyche.

"The objective of studying the Kabbalah is to be skilled for work in the Internal Worlds... One that does not comprehend remains confused in the Internal Worlds. Kabbalah is the basis in order to understand the language of these worlds." - Samael Aun Weor, *The Initiatic Path in the Arcana of Tarot and Kabbalah*

Karma: (Sanskrit, literally "deed"; derived from kri, "to do...") The Law of Cause and Effect. "Be not deceived; God is not mocked: for whatsoever a man soweth, that shall he also reap." - Galatians 6:7

Kundabuffer organ: "In ancient times (due to a certain mistake performed by some sacred individuals) humanity developed the negative side of the Sexual Center, its tenebrous Luciferic aspect. When the electronic sexual fire is directed downwards into the atomic infernos of the human being, it becomes the abominable Kundabuffer organ, the tail of Satan. Fortunately, after its development, that Luciferic organ vanished from humanity; nevertheless, its fatal consequences still remain. It is urgent to know that the disastrous consequences of the abominable Kundabuffer organ remained deposited within the five cylinders of the human machine. It is indispensable to know that the evil consequences of the Abominable Kundabuffer organ constitute the Lunar ego, the pluralized I." - Samael Aun Weor, *The Doomed Aryan Race*. For a full explanation, see *The Elimination of Satan's Tail* by the same author.

Kundalini: "Kundalini, the serpent power or mystic fire, is the primordial energy or Sakti that lies dormant or sleeping in the Muladhara Chakra, the centre of the body. It is called the serpentine or annular power on account of serpentine form. It is an electric fiery occult power, the great pristine force which underlies all organic and inorganic matter. Kundalini is the cosmic power in individual bodies. It is not a material force like electricity, magnetism, centripetal or centrifugal force. It is a spiritual potential Sakti or cosmic power. In reality it has no form. [...] O Divine Mother Kundalini, the Divine Cosmic Energy that is hidden in men! Thou art Kali, Durga, Adisakti, Rajarajeswari, Tripurasundari, Maha-Lakshmi, Maha-Sarasvati! Thou hast put on all these names and forms. Thou hast manifested as Prana, electricity, force, magnetism, cohesion, gravitation in this universe. This whole universe rests in Thy bosom. Crores of salutations unto thee. O Mother of this world! Lead me on to open the Sushumna Nadi and take Thee along the Chakras to Sahasrara Chakra and to merge myself in Thee and Thy consort, Lord Siva. Kundalini Yoga is that Yoga which treats of Kundalini Sakti, the six centres of spiritual energy (Shat Chakras), the arousing of the sleeping Kundalini Sakti and its union with Lord Siva in Sahasrara Chakra, at the crown of the head. This is an exact science. This is also known as Laya Yoga. The six centres are pierced (Chakra Bheda) by the passing of Kundalini Sakti to the top of the head. 'Kundala' means 'coiled'. Her form is like a coiled serpent. Hence the name Kundalini." - Swami Sivananda, *Kundalini Yoga*

Law of the Talion: The lex talionis (Latin for "Law of Retaliation") of Exodus 21:23-25. "An eye for an eye, a tooth for a tooth."

Level of Being: "The level of Being of the drunkard is different from that of the abstemious one, and the level of Being of the prostitute is different from that of the virgin... If we imagine the numerous rungs of a ladder which extends itself upwards, vertically... Unquestionably, we find ourselves on any one of those rungs. On lower rungs will be people worse than us, and on the higher rungs persons better than us will be found." See *Revolutionary Psychology* by the same author.

Logos: (Greek, "word") In Greek and Hebrew metaphysics, the unifying principle of the world. The central idea of the Logos is that it links God and man, hence any system in which the Logos plays a part is monistic. The Logos is the manifested deity of every nation and people; the outward expression or the effect of the cause which is ever concealed. Thus, speech is the Logos of thought; hence it is aptly translated as the Verb, the Word. The First Logos is the Father, the sephiroth Kether; the Second Logos is the Son, the sephiroth Chochmah, and the Third Logos is the Holy Spirit, the sephiroth Binah. These three are one; the tri-unity.

Mahamanvantara: (Sanskrit) "Great Cosmic Day." A period of activity, as opposed to a Mahapralaya, a cosmic night or period of rest.

Mantra: (Sanskrit, literally "mind protection") A sacred word or sound. The use of sacred words and sounds is universal throughout all religions and mystical traditions, because the root of all creation is in the Great Breath or the Word, the Logos. "In the beginning was the Word..."

Master: Like many terms related to spirituality, this one is grossly misunderstood. Samael Aun Weor wrote while describing the Germanic Edda, "In this Genesis of creation we discover Sexual Alchemy. The Fire fecundated the cold waters of chaos. The masculine principle Alfadur fecundated the feminine principle Niffleheim, dominated by Surtur (the Darkness), to bring forth life. That is how Ymir is born, the father of the giants, the Internal God of every human being, the Master." Therefore, the Master is the Innermost, Atman, the Father.

"The only one who is truly great is the Spirit, the Innermost. We, the intellectual animals, are leaves that the wind tosses about... No student of occultism is a Master. True Masters are only those who have reached the

Fifth Initiation of Major Mysteries. Before the Fifth Initiation nobody is a Master." - Samael Aun Weor, *The Perfect Matrimony*

Materialist: In the esoteric sciences, a "materialist" is one who only believes in what his five senses can tell him, thus he relies exclusively on the data of the sensory, third dimensional world. This type of person has no understanding of the superior senses or the superior dimensions, and thus is limited to what he can perceive physically. As C.W. Leadbeter said, "It is one of the commonest of mistakes to consider that the limit of our power of perception is also the limit of all there is to see."

Meditation: "When the esoterist submerges himself into meditation, what he seeks is information." - Samael Aun Weor

"It is urgent to know how to meditate in order to comprehend any psychic aggregate, or in other words, any psychological defect. It is indispensable to know how to work with all our heart and with all our soul, if we want the elimination to occur." - Samael Aun Weor, *The Pistis Sophia Unveiled*

"1. The Gnostic must first attain the ability to stop the course of his thoughts, the capacity to not think. Indeed, only the one who achieves that capacity will hear the Voice of the Silence.

"2. When the Gnostic disciple attains the capacity to not think, then he must learn to concentrate his thoughts on only one thing.

"3. The third step is correct meditation. This brings the first flashes of the new consciousness into the mind.

"4. The fourth step is contemplation, ecstasy or Samadhi. This is the state of Turiya (perfect clairvoyance). - Samael Aun Weor, *The Perfect Matrimony*

Mental Body: One of the seven bodies of the human being. Related to Netzach, the seventh sephirah of the Tree of Life; corresponds to the fifth dimension.

"The mental body is a material organism, yet it is not the physical organism. The mental body has its ultra-biology and its internal pathology, which is completely unknown to the present men of science." - Samael Aun Weor, *The Revolution of Beelzebub*

Monad: (Latin) From monas, "unity; a unit, monad." The Monad is the Being, the Innermost, our own inner Spirit.

"We must distinguish between Monads and Souls. A Monad, in other words, a Spirit, is; a Soul is acquired. Distinguish between the Monad of a world and the Soul of a world; between the Monad of a human and the Soul of a human; between the Monad of an ant and the Soul of an ant. The human organism, in final synthesis, is constituted by billions and trillions of infinitesimal Monads. There are several types and orders of primary elements of all existence, of every organism, in the manner of germs of all the phenomena of nature; we can call the latter Monads, employing the term of Leibnitz, in the absence of a more descriptive term to indicate the simplicity of the simplest existence. An atom, as a vehicle of action, corresponds to each of these genii or Monads. The Monads attract each other, combine, transform themselves, giving form to every organism, world, micro-organism, etc. Hierarchies exist among the Monads; the Inferior Monads must obey the Superior ones that is the Law. Inferior Monads belong to the Superior ones. All the trillions of Monads that animate the human organism have to obey the owner, the chief, the Principal Monad. The regulating Monad, the Primordial Monad permits the activity of all of its subordinates inside the human organism, until the time indicated by the Law of Karma." - Samael Aun Weor, *The Esoteric Treatise of Hermetic Astrology*

"(The number) one is the Monad, the Unity, Iod-Heve or Jehovah, the Father who is in secret. It is the Divine Triad that is not incarnated within a Master who has not killed the ego. He is Osiris, the same God, the Word." - Samael Aun Weor, *Tarot and Kabbalah*

"When spoken of, the Monad is referred to as Osiris. He is the one who has to Self-realize Himself... Our own particular Monad needs us and we need it. Once, while speaking with my Monad, my Monad told me, 'I am self-realizing Thee; what I am doing, I am doing for Thee.' Otherwise, why are we living? The Monad wants to Self-realize and that is why we are here. This is our objective." - Samael Aun Weor, *Tarot and Kabbalah*

"The Monads or Vital Genii are not exclusive to the physical organism; within the atoms of the Internal Bodies there are found imprisoned many orders and categories of living Monads. The existence of any physical or supersensible, Angelic or Diabolical, Solar or Lunar body, has billions and trillions of Monads as their foundation." - Samael Aun Weor, *The Esoteric Treatise of Hermetic Astrology*

Monera: The taxonomic kingdom that comprises the prokaryotes (bacteria and cyanobacteria). Prokaryotes are single-celled organisms that lack a membrane-bound nucleus and usually lack membrane-bound organelles (mitochondria, chloroplasts). They have a small ring of DNA as their genetic material and reproduce asexually. In the theories of Haeckel, all life presumably arose from a singular root Monera, afloat in a primordial sea.

Moon Earth: The author is referring to the life that flourished on the planet that we now call the Moon. For more information, see *The Doomed Aryan Race.*

Natural Selection: The process by which forms of life having traits that better enable them to adapt to specific environmental pressures, as predators, changes in climate, or competition for food or mates, will tend to survive and reproduce in greater numbers than others of their kind, thus ensuring the perpetuation of those favorable traits in succeeding generations. Cf. "survival of the fittest."

Ontogeny: The development or developmental history of an individual organism. Ernst von Haeckel proposed that "ontogeny recapitulates phylogeny." This jargon, when translated into English, asserts that as an embryo develops it passes through stages that are equivalent to the adult forms of its ancestors. For example, according to Haeckel, a human embryo would pass through a stage in which it has features of an adult fish, then features of an adult amphibian, and so forth. Gnostic anthropology observes the three lower kingdoms in the development of the human fetus, a recapitulation of the millions of years of the evolution of the consciousness as it ascended up the evolutionary path from mineral to plant to animal, until finally achieving its goal: the opportunity of a human birth. See *Gnostic Anthropology* by Samael Aun Weor.

Particular Characteristic Psychological Feature: Also known as the Chief Feature.

Permanent Center of Consciousness/Gravity: See *Revolutionary Psychology*.

Phylogeny: 1. the development or evolution of a particular group of organisms. 2. the evolutionary history of a group of organisms, esp. as depicted in a family tree.

POSCLA: Partido Socialista Cristiano Latino Americano (Latin American Christian Socialist Party) A political action group formed by Samael Aun Weor in Latin America that he later dissolved because the ego was too strong in its members.

Protist: With this term the author is referring to those who subscribe to the theory that all life arose from one simple organism. In materialistic science, a protist is any of various one-celled organisms, classified in the kingdom Protista, that are either free-living or aggregated into simple colonies and that have diverse reproductive and nutritional modes, including the protozoans, eukaryotic algae, and slime molds. Some classification schemes also include the fungi and the more primitive bacteria and blue-green algae or may distribute the organisms between the kingdoms Plantae and Animalia according to dominant characteristics.

Samadhi: (Sanskrit) Literally means "union" or "combination" and its Tibetan equivilent means "adhering to that which is profound and definitive," or ting nge dzin, meaning "To hold unwaveringly, so there is no movement." Related terms include satori, ecstasy, manteia, etc. Samadhi is a state of consciousness. In the west, the term is used to describe an ecstatic state of consciousness in which the Essence escapes the painful limitations of the mind (the "I") and therefore experiences what is real: the Being, the Great Reality. There are many levels of Samadhi. In the sutras and tantras the term Samadhi has a much broader application whose precise interpretation depends upon which school and teaching is using it.

"Ecstasy is not a nebulous state, but a transcendental state of wonderment, which is associated with perfect mental clarity." - Samael Aun Weor, *The Elimination of Satan's Tail*

Samsara: (Sanskrit; Tibetan khorwa) Cyclic, conditioned existence whose defining characteristic is suffering. It is contrasted with nirvana.

Sensual Mind: From Gnostic psychology, one of the three types of mind. "Unquestionably, the Sensual Mind develops its basic concepts via external sensory perceptions. Under these conditions the Sensual Mind is terribly crude and materialistic. It cannot accept anything which has not been physically demonstrated. Since the fundamental concepts of the Sensual Mind are based on external sensory data, undoubtedly it can know nothing about what is real, about the truth, about the mysteries of life and death, about the Soul and the Spirit, etc. For the rogues of the intellect, totally trapped by their external senses and incarcerated within the basic concepts of the Sensual Mind, our esoteric studies are lunacy." - Samael Aun Weor, *The Great Rebellion*

Separation: Samael Aun Weor wrote, "The fire of comprehension reduces to dust the decay of the past. Many students of Psychology, (when trying to achieve the silence and quietude of the mind) analyze their subconsciousness and commit the mistake of dividing themselves between analyzer and analyzed, intellect and subconsciousness, subject and object, perceiver and perceived." In essence, Samael is indicating the tendency to say, "That element (the subconscious one) is not ME." This is a mistake. Since the mind is the den of the subconsciousness and since the mind always struggles between the opposites, when we try to achieve the silence and quietude of the mind we have to analyze the subconsciousness without committing the mistake of dividing ourselves between the opposites: analyzer and analyzed, intellect and subconsciousness, subject and object, perceiver and perceived. The Truth, the Satori, Samadhi, is attained in the silence and quietude of the mind by acquiring the INTEGRATION of our consciousness in one whole. If a division exists within ourselves, then the whole (the Tality or Totality), the Satori, is impossible.

However, if we are analyzing the ego in order to annihilate it, we have to divide ourselves into Observer and Observed (we have to divide the light from the darkness) in order to not fascinate ourselves with our different psychological aggregates, that is, in order not to fall into the fascination of that particular aggregate of lust, anger, etc., and not to fall into our ego's temptation. One divides the ATTENTION: being aware that what one sees (through visualization) is part of the one who is seeing (the consciousness). Therefore, one must divide one's attention in order to separate from temptation, but maintain awareness of the duality of that phenomena. This apparent contradiction is a position of attentiveness that cannot be understood by the dualistic mind. One must practice meditation and the perfection of attention in order to comprehend.

Self-observation: An exercise of attention, in which one learns to become an indifferent observer of one's own psychological process. True Self-observation is an active work of directed attention, without the interference of thought.

"We need attention intentionally directed towards the interior of our own selves. This is not a passive attention. Indeed, dynamic attention proceeds from the side of the observer, while thoughts and emotions belong to the side which is observed." - Samael Aun Weor, *Revolutionary Psychology*

Self-realization: The achievement of perfect knowledge. This phrase is better stated as, "The realization of the Innermost Self," or "The realization of the true nature of self." At the ultimate level, this is the experiential, conscious knowledge of the Absolute, which is synonymous with Emptiness, Shunyata, or Non-being.

Self-remembering: A state of active consciousness, controlled by will, that begins with awareness of being here and now. This state has many levels (see: Consciousness). True Self-remembering occurs without thought or mental processing: it is a state of conscious perception and includes the remembrance of the inner Being.

Seven planets: In esoteric science, the seven primary planets are the Moon, Mercury, Venus, the Sun, Mars, Jupiter and Saturn. These are the embodiment and expression of the Law of Seven which organizes all creation. Of course, esoteric science has long stated that there are more than seven planets in this solar system.

Solar Bodies: The physical, vital, astral, mental, and casual bodies that are created through the beginning stages of Alchemy/Tantra and that provide a basis for existence in their corresponding levels of nature, just as the physical body does in the physical world. These bodies or vehicles are superior due to being created out of Solar (Christic) Energy, as opposed to the inferior, lunar bodies we receive from nature. Also known as the Wedding Garment (Christianity), the Merkabah (Kabbalah), To Soma Heliakon (Greek), and Sahu (Egyptian).

"All the Masters of the White Lodge, the Angels, Archangels, Thrones, Seraphim, Virtues, etc., etc., etc. are garbed with the Solar Bodies. Only those who have Solar Bodies have the Being incarnated. Only someone who possesses the Being is an authentic Human Being." - Samael Aun Weor, *The Esoteric Treatise of Hermetic Astrology*

Thelema: (Greek) Willpower.

Three-brained biped: Gnostic Psychology recognizes that humanoids actually have three centers of intelligence within: an intellectual brain, an emotional brain, and a motor/instinctive/sexual brain. These are not physical brains; they are divisions of organized activity. Each one functions and operates independent of the others, and each one has a host of jobs and duties that only it can accomplish. Of course, in modern humanity the three brains are grossly out of balance and used incorrectly. See *Revolutionary Psychology* by the author.

Index

Glorian Publishing is a non-profit publisher dedicated to spreading the sacred universal doctrine to suffering humanity. All of our works are made possible by the kindness and generosity of sponsors. If you would like to make a tax-deductible donation, you may send it to the address below, or visit our website for other alternatives. If you would like to sponsor the publication of a book, please contact us at 877-726-2359 or help@ gnosticteachings.org.

Glorian Publishing
PO Box 110225
Brooklyn, NY 11211 US
Phone: 877-726-2359

VISIT US ONLINE AT:

glorian.info
gnosticbooks.org
gnosticteachings.org
gnosticradio.org
gnosticstore.org